RECLAIMING AUTHENTICITY

UNEARTH YOUR TRUE SELF AND BUILD AN EQUITABLE CLASSROOM

JACOBÉ BELL

RESHMA RAMKELLAWAN

Solution Tree | Press

a division of
Solution Tree

AI output featured in figures 2.1 and 2.2 generated with the assistance of Gemini.

555 North Morton Street
Bloomington, IN 47404
800.733.6786 (toll free) / 812.336.7700
FAX: 812.336.7790

email: info@SolutionTree.com
SolutionTree.com

Visit **go.SolutionTree.com/diversityandequity** to download the free reproducibles in this book.

Printed in the United States of America

FSC
www.fsc.org
MIX
Paper | Supporting responsible forestry
FSC® C008955

Library of Congress Cataloging-in-Publication Data

Names: Bell, Jacobē, author. | Ramkellawan-Arteaga, Reshma, author.
Title: Reclaiming authenticity : unearth your true self and build an
    equitable classroom / Jacobē Bell, Reshma Ramkellawan.
Description: Bloomington, IN : Solution Tree Press, [2025] | Includes
    bibliographical references and index.
Identifiers: LCCN 2024041394 (print) | LCCN 2024041395 (ebook) | ISBN
    9781954631670 (paperback) | ISBN 9781954631687 (ebook)
Subjects: LCSH: Educational equalization. | Authenticity (Philosophy) in
    education. | Social justice and education. | Discrimination in
    education. | Reflective education.
Classification: LCC LC213 .B44 2025 (print) | LCC LC213 (ebook) | DDC
    379.2/6--dc23/eng/20241009
LC record available at https://lccn.loc.gov/2024041394
LC ebook record available at https://lccn.loc.gov/2024041395

Solution Tree
Jeffrey C. Jones, CEO
Edmund M. Ackerman, President

Solution Tree Press
President and Publisher: Douglas M. Rife
Associate Publishers: Todd Brakke and Kendra Slayton
Editorial Director: Laurel Hecker
Art Director: Rian Anderson
Copy Chief: Jessi Finn
Production Editor: Paige Duke
Acquisitions Editors: Carol Collins and Hilary Goff
Content Development Specialist: Amy Rubenstein
Associate Editors: Sarah Ludwig and Elijah Oates
Editorial Assistant: Madison Chartier

We begin this book by offering gratitude.

- Gratitude for all the teachers and educators we've worked with who allowed us to learn beside them.
- Gratitude for all those who've pushed our thinking.
- Gratitude for all the students who have been our greatest teachers.
- Gratitude for our families who have helped keep us grounded.
- Gratitude for our peers and colleagues who have acted as thought partners.

Without you, this book would not be. We would not be who we are. Thank you.

ACKNOWLEDGMENTS

Solution Tree Press would like to thank the following reviewers:

Gerald Dessus
Director of Diversity, Equity, and
   Inclusion
The Philadelphia School
Philadelphia, Pennsylvania

Jenna Fanshier
Sixth-Grade Teacher
Hesston Middle School
Hesston, Kansas

Kelly Hilliard
GATE Mathematics Instructor NBCT
Darrell C. Swope Middle School
Reno, Nevada

Teresa Kinley
Humanities Teacher
Calgary, Alberta, Canada

Amy Kochensparger
Science Teacher
Eaton High School
Eaton, Ohio

Louis Lim
Principal
Bur Oak Secondary School
Markham, Ontario, Canada

Shanna Martin
Middle School Teacher and
   Instructional Coach
School District of Lomira
Lomira, Wisconsin

Demetra Mylonas
Education Researcher
Headwater Learning Foundation
Calgary, Alberta, Canada

Laurie Warner
PLC Trainer
Deer Valley Unified School District
Phoenix, Arizona

Visit **go.SolutionTree.com/diversityandequity**
to download the free reproducibles in this book.

TABLE OF CONTENTS

Reproducibles are in italics.

CHAPTER 2

CHAPTER 3

CHAPTER 4

CHAPTER 5

CHAPTER 6

ABOUT THE AUTHORS

Jacobē Bell is a seasoned change agent with over eighteen years of diverse experience as a National Board Certified Teacher, instructional coach, educational consultant, and network administrator in both public and charter school environments. Committed to fostering sustainable and equitable practices in education, Jacobē firmly believes in creating asset-based environments where joy and student voices flourish. Her experience spans coaching principals, teachers, and network teams; teaching students from elementary to graduate levels; and designing culturally responsive curriculum and professional development sessions.

Jacobē's influence extends beyond the classroom, as she has shared her insights at prestigious academic conferences, including the National Council of Teachers of English (NCTE), the World Education Research Association (WERA), the American Educational Research Association (AERA), the Carnegie Summit, and the National Alliance for Partnerships in Equity (NAPE). She has also been a proud member of NCTE and AERA. Her expertise has graced the pages of respected publications such as *The Learning Professional*, *The 74*, and the *International Journal of Qualitative Studies in Education*. Her research and speaking engagements encompass a wide array of topics, from equity-centered schooling to culturally responsive classrooms and strategic school improvement.

Jacobē holds a bachelor's degree from Stanford University, received a master's degree in urban education from Mercy College, and is currently pursuing her doctorate at Teachers College, Columbia University, in New York, specializing in curriculum and teaching. Her professional interests include humanizing pedagogies, student-centered learning, curriculum design, asset-based teaching, culturally responsive teaching, teacher preparation, and leadership development.

Reshma Ramkellawan is an educational consultant and cofounder of Equity Consulting Group who brings a wealth of experience and passion to her role. Beyond her instructional coaching duties, she serves as a part-time lecturer at Rutgers University, guiding future educators in crafting dynamic curricular experiences. Reshma's diverse background includes stints as an English teacher, department leader, and school administrator in both New York City and Florida's public school systems. She began her journey in education as an intern at a Montessori school, paving the way for roles as a substitute teacher and department leader. She emphasizes the importance of authenticity and empathy in creating a nurturing learning environment. Inspired by the educators who shaped her own path, Reshma remains dedicated to uplifting students who share her background. Her multifaceted career reflects her unwavering commitment to empowering students and educators alike.

Reshma is a member of NCTE and AERA, and she currently serves on the College Section Steering Committee for NCTE. She was the secretary for the Research on the Education of Asian and Pacific Americans special interest group for AERA from 2020 to 2022. Reshma believes in the power of building the capacity of all educators. The scope of her research, publications, and public speaking ranges from curriculum and assessment to design, strategic planning for intentional school improvement, improvement science, and culturally responsive practices.

Reshma received a bachelor's degree with honors in English education from the University of Central Florida. She received a master of arts in curriculum and teaching, a master of education in English education, and a doctorate in the teaching of English from Teachers College, Columbia University, in New York.

To book Jacobē Bell or Reshma Ramkellawan Hanlin for professional development, contact pd@solutiontree.com.

FOREWORD

To teach in a manner that respects and cares for
the souls of our students is essential if we are to
provide the necessary conditions where learning
can most deeply and intimately begin.

—bell hooks

For educators, the path to the classroom is intricately woven with personal stories, transformative moments, unconscious assumptions, and our hopes for the students we are called to teach. Many of us choose teaching because of a teacher who saw us and affirmed our potential, or because we want to fill the gaps left by the harm and neglect we may have experienced in our own educational journey. This decision to teach is deeply intertwined with our identities—yet too often we move through teacher education programs without being asked to examine those identities or how they inform our teaching. I wonder: *What happens when our identities remain unexamined? When the layers of who we are—our assumptions, biases, and values—go unacknowledged, unchallenged, and unhealed?*

Reclaiming Authenticity: Unearth Your True Self and Build an Equitable Classroom seeks to answer these questions and calls educators into the courageous, transformative work of reflection that I call the Archaeology of Self™. This process—one of excavation, discovery, and authenticity—is fundamental to equitable teaching. It demands that we peel back the layers of our experiences, examine the beliefs and biases that shape our pedagogy, and commit to a practice rooted in authenticity, care, and love. It is not easy work. It is uncomfortable, messy, and complex. But it is the most necessary work we can do; without it, we risk perpetuating harm, silencing the genius of our students, and neglecting the humanity of every student.

This book is a gift to educators, and it is crafted with careful intention. Jacobē and Reshma invite us to explore our identities, interrogate systemic inequities, and reimagine what is possible for ourselves and our students. They challenge us to transgress the limits of the status quo—an educational system that often marginalizes, standardizes, and dehumanizes—and to step into a praxis of teaching that centers humanity, equity, and liberation.

The sequence of chapters has been thoughtfully designed to take readers on a journey of change. Chapter 1 begins with the foundational work of embracing authenticity, urging educators to explore their identities and recognize how cultural competence shapes teaching practices. Chapter 2 expands this exploration to include intersectionality, examining how the interplay of race, class, gender, and other identities informs our pedagogical approaches. Chapter 3 offers an unflinching look at systemic inequities in schools, challenging readers to understand the structural forces that shape educational spaces. The book then moves into the relational. Chapter 4 explores how an educator's authenticity—or lack thereof—affects their relationships with students, curriculum, and the broader school community. Chapter 5 turns inward, inviting readers to uncover how schools, and educators themselves, can perpetuate internalized harm. Finally, Chapter 6 dares educators to dream boldly, using Afrofuturism as a lens to envision classrooms where possibility, liberation, and humanity are at the center. Each chapter calls on educators to do the work of excavating what shapes us as individuals, as teachers, and as participants in this education system. The reflective activities and strategies presented in the book are not merely tools—they are invitations to change how we teach and better understand why our authentic selves matter in the classroom. As you read this beautiful and innovative book, consider the words of Audre Lorde: "When we speak, we are afraid our words will not be heard nor welcomed. But when we are silent, we are still afraid. So it is better to speak" (p. 28). This book encourages us to speak—to confront the internal and external forces (with authenticity)—forces that can help us act with clarity, courage, and love.

The guiding principle of this book is clear: authenticity transforms. From the exploration of The Value of Authenticity (chapter 1) to the visionary aspirations in Dreams of an Authentic Future (chapter 6), this text weaves together individual reflection and systemic change. It challenges educators to embrace their "ratchedemic" sensibilities, as Dr. Christopher Emdin (2021b) describes, and to recognize that authenticity is not only personal but also communal. It calls on us to nurture our own identities while cultivating relationships that affirm the humanity and genius of our students.

Through the lens of the Archaeology of Self™, we learn that every interaction, lesson, and decision reflect our histories, values, and beliefs. Jacobé and Reshma ask us to interrogate how unexamined assumptions affect our practice, how our authenticity—or its absence—impacts our students, and what we must unlearn to create classrooms that center humanity and brilliance. Authenticity is not just a goal; it is a practice, one that demands community, relationship, and accountability.

To the educators reading this book: I invite you to step into this journey. The work is lifelong. By engaging in the work that Jacobē and Reshma offer, we can move toward the deep self-reflection that is necessary to create schools that not only educate but also affirm, heal, and liberate. This book offers educators a road map, a mirror, and a guide. Through their wisdom, and your commitment, we can begin to reimagine and realize an education system that centers authenticity, equity, and love.

Let us dig, together.

Yolanda Sealey-Ruiz, PhD
Teachers College, Columbia University
New York City

INTRODUCTION

For most educators, the decision to enter the practice of teaching is grounded in a formative educational experience. Whether it was playing school as a child and teaching others or having an inspiring teacher, the decision to become a pedagogue is influenced by our experiences and unconscious beliefs. Once we get into the field, our peers can influence the development of our teaching identity and ideology around schooling.

Saela was the first teacher I, Jacobē, became enamored with. As a first-year teacher, I shared a classroom with her and delighted in watching her teach during my off periods. Sitting in the back of our classroom while grading papers, I marveled at her creativity, engagement, and authenticity and more largely, at how she facilitated learning. She facilitated author study book clubs that had her fifth graders on the edge of their seats. She wrote and included her stories in lessons in ways that engaged learners and made them smile. One of my favorite things she did was reader's theater. She was my aspiration and inspiration. But five years later, she was a completely different teacher. The joy and spark was gone from her teaching. I asked her what happened. Basically, her teaching style didn't fit the mold of her administration's expectations. They expected her to teach gradual release lessons using the basal reader. This killed her creativity and motivation; she was no longer able to bring her authenticity into the classroom.

For me, Reshma, I wanted to be a teacher for as long as I can remember. As an early reader and firstborn child, it fell on my shoulders to teach everyone else—my younger sister and my many cousins—to read. School was fairly easy for me until I reached middle school. My teachers, while well intentioned, often engaged in practices that were harmful to the soul. I distinctly remember my second-grade teacher saying that I was not "smart" enough. By middle school, I had to advocate for placement in honors classes because no one noticed my capability. When I was accepted to one of the most elite public magnet high schools in New York State, my eighth-grade science teacher told me I was accepted to fulfill a quota. The one ray of light in the chaos of school and at times my home life was Mrs. Dawn Bailey-Peaks.

She was kind, she was caring, and she made reading from an anthology enjoyable. Years later, I still search for her on social media. I haven't been able to find her and wouldn't be surprised if she has left education. She showed up for her students in ways that affirmed their humanity. She was unapologetically herself and encouraged her students to be the same.

In this book, we seek to encourage and support teachers in their pedagogical journey. We invite you to think about the ways we as educators have been consciously and unconsciously molded to view education and the implications for the students we teach. The book deconstructs ways in which we can cultivate authentic, human-centered teaching practices through intentional reflection and mindfulness.

This book was born out of our frustration of seeing teachers asked to teach divorced from their identities, expected to leave who they are at the door. It is birthed out of seeing the current education system inadvertently harm both educators and students. It is birthed out of a vision to see schools and learning grounded in culture, affirm students' and educators' humanity, and center healing, love, and liberation. It is birthed from our experiences doing change work with hundreds of educators. By delving into the complexities of our socialization and confronting uncomfortable truths, we hope to empower readers to become agents of positive change, driving toward a more inclusive and just society for all.

MEET THE AUTHORS

I am Jacobē Bell. I am a sister, a daughter, an encourager, a mentor, a sunshine chaser, a coach, a scholar, a salsa dancer, an educator, a change agent, and a Black woman living with a primarily invisible disability. I have taught grades 4–9 in both public and charter schools. I am a National Board Certified Teacher, a former literacy coach, and a former director of curriculum and instruction. I currently run a network of sixteen public schools. I wear a few hats, but one of the ones I enjoy the most is developing and mentoring a team of educational consultants who work in our network of schools across New York City. I also consult as I continue to walk the walk and talk the talk.

I am Reshma Ramkellawan. I am a first-generation Indo-Guyanese American. I am the daughter of two hardworking immigrants, both of whom have high school diplomas. Growing up, they impressed on my sister and me the importance of education and how this system would serve as the great equalizer. Since becoming a mother to two children—one of them highly sensitive and intellectually gifted—I've taken a critical look at my own practice and the ways in which schooling has shaped my ideologies. Professionally, I am a former seventh-grade English language arts (ELA) teacher, grade team leader, and school administrator. I've been an educator since I was seventeen, when I began working in a Montessori school on the Lower East Side of Manhattan. These days, I am a part-time lecturer at Rutgers University and an educational consultant to several school districts and over seven schools.

For this book, we draw most heavily on our facilitation, coaching, consulting, and leading, as well as our experience as thought partners across New York City public and charter schools. We have been facilitating and coaching school change work since 2011 and 2013, respectively. But we started engaging in change work much earlier in both high school and college.

We are sister-scholars, sister-colleagues, and sister-friends. We first met in 2011 through our teaching experiences in a charter network. Although we taught and mentored in different schools, as women of color we connected. Our paths crossed again at a nonprofit consulting firm, where we connected as a handful of people of color in a primarily White institution. It was at this job that our friendship blossomed. As two women of color, we see the beautiful parts of education and the sordid underbelly. We have been thought partners in one another's work and have created a safe place for each other to be vulnerable about the challenges facing students and educators of color and the weight of carrying and navigating change work. It is these interactions that undergird how we came together to write this book. As sister-colleagues, we saw the layers of societal socialization that inform schooling in America. Our decision to collaborate on writing this book is rooted in a deep understanding of the challenges educators and students face and our deep commitment to educational justice.

LOOKING BACK TO MOVE FORWARD

Sankofa is a term from the Twi language that means, "It is not taboo [for you] to go back for what you forgot (or left behind)" (Stockton University, n.d.). *Sankofa* embodies the idea of learning from the past, understanding one's history, and using that knowledge to move forward and make positive progress. *Sankofa* encourages people to reflect on their cultural and historical heritage to gain insights for their current and future actions. It is about looking back to move forward, much like the idea of learning from the past. Similarly, in Sanskrit, the concept of *Svadhyaya* refers to the idea of elevating one's self and others through perpetual self-reflection. *Svadhyaya* emphasizes the importance of understanding one's inner self and fulfilling one's unique purpose or duty in life. This also involves self-reflection and drawing from inner resources to make choices that align with one's true nature. Both these concepts share common themes of self-awareness, introspection, and learning from the past to inform present and future actions.

This book is meant to prompt reflection and introspection. Our book is about you. It is about the ways in which education has affirmed and harmed you. It challenges us as educators to peek beneath the veneer and probe problematic racist ideology because it exists in all systems, particularly schools. It challenges us to explore the historical aspects of self, schooling, and society and their effects on us as well as our teaching and learning. This book prompts us to think about the ways in which we unintentionally harm students because of our own lived harm. This book challenges all educators to do better and be better. This book prompts us to consider the ways in which our authenticity has been molded by who we seek to be and what the world has told us we should be.

This process requires us to consider the ways in which racism has influenced our worldview and perceptions of authenticity. We want educators to ask, "How might I unintentionally perpetuate racist ideology due to my lived experiences and the conditioning of Whiteness as espoused by society? How might these internalized constructs influence how I engage my students?" This book aspires to help educators move from unintentional harm to intentional practice grounded in cultural competence. To do this, educators must examine themselves beyond a superficial level. We must confront the intricate ways in which racist ideologies have given rise to unjust systems that harm all members of society. We dream of a different future than our past—for educators and students alike. In this book, we aim to cultivate manageable and meaningful pathways for ensuring that authenticity is the focal point of the classroom, therefore centering humanity.

To do this work, it's critical to acknowledge federal and local systems, policies, and practices that are deeply entrenched in racist ideologies and White supremacy that deny human beings' diverse identities. As one example, consider legislation and rhetoric that targets marginalized groups while failing to acknowledge historical injustices and promote equitable education. Specifically, legislation was passed in numerous states in 2022 and 2023 to prohibit the use of texts that center the experiences of marginalized groups such as religious and ethnic minorities. The state also passed similar legislation targeting the discussion of America's racial history. When confronted with these legal quandaries, teachers must stifle elements of their own identities and beliefs for fear of repercussion. These laws are designed to ensure that particular groups of people (both teachers and students) are not allowed a presence within classroom environments.

Our focus primarily centers on the discourse of racism and how it impacts teachers' ability to be authentic, yet we are acutely aware that the principles and strategies we explore extend to people advocating against ableism, fighting for LGBTQIA+ rights, and championing individual autonomy. This book transcends mere surface discussions, compelling educators to confront the influences that have shaped their perspectives and attitudes. Ultimately, our goal is to prompt readers to engage in meaningful conversations about racism, to critically evaluate the societal structures that perpetuate inequities, and to recognize the shared responsibility educators have in dismantling these systems. While wading through these tricky topics, we encourage you to ask yourself: "How does this impact my ability to be an authentic educator?"

Saela, who you read about earlier, lost her spark when she was asked to teach within the lines drawn by her administration. She was expected to leave her identity at the door, and it stymied her teaching in ways that harmed students. As we reflect about the self, the system, societal expectations, and history, we as educators can learn not only about ourselves but also about the world around us. If we fail to engage in reflection, we can unwittingly cause harm to our students and other educators. Professor Yolanda Sealey-Ruiz (n.d.) encourages us to peel back the layer of self:

> Simply put, the archaeology of self—like an archaeological dig, like a digging deep, like a peeling back of layers—is for teachers to really think deeply about how these issues live in them. Issues of race, issues of class, issues of religious practices. . . . to teach someone or to be open to someone (and that really is what teaching is, to be open to other people's stories), you have to know your own story. You have to be aware of who you are, what you bring to the classroom, how you're going to interact with the children that you are there to serve. And if you're not open with your story, if you do not think deeply about how these issues live in you, you would just exact harm. You will traumatize. . . . And so this kind of deep work I believe has to be done before we can even begin to have someone take up theoretical practices or to examine your pedagogy.

By reflecting on the complexity of our identity, we connect with our inner self to teach with greater authenticity and to heal the harm within us rather than perpetuate it to our students. Teachers who embrace their true, authentic selves and are aware of their identity tend to adopt greater cultural competency that allows for culturally proficient learning experiences.

ABOUT THIS BOOK

Although each chapter in this book is self-contained, we've crafted the sequence of chapters with intention so that the ideas build on each other. Each chapter enriches the last, taking readers on a learning and reflection journey like stepping stones. We ask that you not skip chapters but read and reflect in the order they appear, as each stepping stone leads readers further into the heart of our collective purpose, which is school and system change work.

Chapter 1 (page 9) delves into the realms of authenticity, urging educators to embrace their genuine selves and to recognize the significant role of cultural competency in shaping their teaching practices.

Chapter 2 (page 25) recognizes the significant role of a teacher's identity, intersectionality, and cultural competence in their journey toward authenticity.

Chapter 3 (page 55) shifts focus to the presence of racist systems within educational institutions. Through this immersive journey, we intend to shed light on the intricate web of systemic inequities that affect our schools.

Chapter 4 (page 83) examines how a teacher's authenticity affects their relationships with students in terms of power dynamics, curriculum, and student identity.

Chapter 5 (page 111) turns to unravelling the multifaceted role of schools in perpetuating internalized harm. We dissect this complex relationship, aiming to uncover the ways in which educational settings can either reinforce or challenge societal norms and biases.

Chapter 6 (page 141) draws on Afrofuturism as a lens for exploring possibility. We consider how teachers envision a future that transcends current limitations, and we challenge educators to dream, innovate, and create spaces that empower all students.

Through each chapter, this book aims to be a transformative guide taking readers on a journey from examining systemic racism to envisioning a future of equitable education. It is our hope that by engaging with these themes, educators will be equipped to enact meaningful change within themselves, their classrooms, and the broader educational landscape.

A NOTE TO THE READER

We acknowledge that education is a profoundly human endeavor. It is a dance of hearts and minds, where educators and students intertwine in a delicate choreography. In this dance, we encounter challenges and struggles that deserve attention. There are moments when we need to question our methods, approaches, and impact on those entrusted in our care. It is during these vulnerable moments that we uncover the seeds of growth and the potential for profound change.

In this book, we invite you to embrace vulnerability and reflect on your journey as an educator with an open heart. We urge you to lean in boldly and courageously, for it is within these spaces of introspection that we gather the strength to challenge the status quo. In this book, we share activities that have helped us on our journeys. If you encounter something you don't like in the book, we encourage you to metabolize those emotions. Don't ignore them; rather, we ask you to embrace them (Bell, 2022). We encourage you to fearlessly confront the tough questions, reevaluate your methods, and explore various perspectives that shape the educational landscape. We acknowledge that there are common systemwide issues and that individual classrooms have specific contextual restrictions. We offer options and strategies that you should apply as relevant.

As you immerse yourself in the chapters of this book, please remember that our pursuit of transformation springs from a profound love for the humanity of educators and students—a love that knows no bounds and steadfastly commits to transformation.

CHAPTER 1

THE VALUE OF AUTHENTICITY

One year I, Jacobē, observed Ms. Xenos, a middle school English teacher I was coaching at the time. She was teaching a lesson on a text, intending for students to make connections to their lived experiences. But instead of focusing on the lesson, students were chatting about off-topic content. Ms. Xenos talked over them to continue with her lesson. When she called for attention, most students stopped talking and listened to her. When she engaged the class in a discussion based on the passage she'd been reading aloud, the students resumed their prior conversations with little regard to focusing on the discussion question. When asked to complete an assignment, most students complied.

In our debrief after her lesson, Ms. Xenos expressed frustration that her well-planned lesson had not taken root. We discussed classroom structures to support learning, such as discussion protocols like letting students talk first in groups before sharing out. We also discussed her facilitation style. I asked, "What connections do you feel to the content? And how do students know how you feel? How might you bring that forth in your classroom?"

Ms. Xenos looked at me, baffled. "I don't know."

I responded, "You seem to be trying to replicate the training videos from your district professional development, which isn't necessarily a bad thing. However, I am left wondering, 'What is your, Ms. Xenos's, teacher persona that feels true to you? What is authentic to you?'"

The uncertainty Ms. Xenos felt about who she was in the classroom based on the training she received, her school's expectations, and navigating the curriculum is not unique to her. Her robotic implementation of the gradual release method, rote implementation of the given questions in the teacher guidebook, and revisions to the lesson based on her school's structure are all subconsciously grounded in her understanding of what others expect of her. It's an experience many teachers share. All the competing interests in schools, the history of teacher education, societal demands,

9

and lived experiences often shape a teacher's identity in the classroom (Danielewicz, 2001; Duff & Uchida, 1997).

In this chapter, we establish a definition of authenticity and explore how our identities outside of the classroom should and do intersect with our teacher identity (Sealey-Ruiz, n.d.). Students can discern a teacher's authenticity (or lack thereof). Powerful learning happens when teachers show up as their authentic selves in the classroom.

Guiding Questions

What is authenticity?

- How might others' expectations dictate how you present yourself in the classroom?
- How are those expectations hurting or helping you as a teacher?

DEFINING AUTHENTICITY

The word *authentic* is thrown around in education, but what does it mean? What does it look and feel like for teachers to bring their authentic selves into the classroom? Authenticity means different things to different people. For some, it may mean "keepin' it real"; for others, it may mean being true to yourself. A teacher's peers and students often perceive them as authentic when their teaching space feels unique to their specific classroom (De Bruyckere & Kirschner, 2016). As master-certified coach Lyn Christian (2021) describes it, "Authenticity means having a keen awareness of who you are and what you stand for, and expressing yourself honestly and consistently to the world."

In this book, we define *authenticity* as being in touch with your inner self so you don't get lost in pleasing others in ways that are detrimental to yourself and your students. It means acknowledging the external factors that have shaped who you are and how you continue to evolve.

This can show up in multiple ways in schools. One example of how we've observed this is when instructional strategies rooted in Afrocentric ways of knowing, such as call and response techniques, fall flat due to a lack of connection or buy-in from students because they're accustomed to Eurocentric instructional strategies. When a strategy doesn't go as expected, it's a great opportunity for the teacher to reflect on what went wrong and use that information to shift their practice. This includes considering questions such as the following:

- "How might my identity interplay with how this instructional strategy worked out?"
- "Is the strategy I am attempting to use something I feel comfortable with? Is it relevant to how I seek to present or show up in the classroom?"
- "Does the way I implemented this strategy align with who I am as an educator?"
- "Did I experience tension while I was planning this strategy, and if so, why did I ignore it?"

Authenticity is not static but ever shifting as a person's multiple identities interact and make meaning. Thus, there are many degrees of authenticity. In other words, authenticity is *created* through interactions. To label an interaction or event as inherently authentic is to oversimplify the construct; authenticity is socially constructed from moment to moment.

In writing this book, we asked students to weigh in on what makes a teacher authentic. Consider some of the most common themes from their responses:

- "The teacher doesn't yell at us."
- "The teacher is honest with us."
- "Sometimes the teacher shares things about their life—like if they are in a bad mood."
- "The teacher understands if we aren't in a good mood or feeling school."
- "Sometimes we don't want to be here, and the teacher doesn't take it personally."

These responses got us thinking about a common theme across how students see their teachers and the process of schooling. There is a subtle power dynamic between students and teachers that can often influence the ways in which educators see their students and vice versa. It is a hierarchical structure that minimizes students' and educators' ability to see each other with full humanity. Examples of this include authoritarian teaching styles, stereotyping, and lacking empathy for one another.

When humanity is stripped away, authenticity goes right along with it (Emdin, 2021). If we as educators are not cognizant of the power we hold because of our position, students become conditioned to assume they do not have power or agency, thereby being stripped of their humanity. The irony of this is the fact that many teachers experience this same sentiment when legislators or district officials pass mandates without soliciting input.

In her inaugural book, Bettina L. Love (2019) writes, "Abolitionist teaching is choosing to engage in the struggle for educational justice knowing that you have the ability and human right to refuse oppression and refuse to oppress others, mainly your students" (p. 11). We believe that subtle shifts in how we see ourselves and our students, even in confined instances, can lead to students and educators feeling validated and seen. Educator Christopher Emdin (2021b) suggests there are seven Buddhist rights to ensure the infusion of authenticity into students' learning experiences: (1) to be here, (2) to feel, (3) to act, (4) to love, (5) to speak, (6) to see, and (7) to know. If you are unsure of how to cultivate authenticity, considering these pillars and whether they are present in your classroom and practice is a helpful starting point. Building on this foundation, we argue that a teacher's authentic self is structured on these seven pillars. It requires an intentional self-awareness that humanizes the educator and student. Undertaking this self-reflection process can be tricky—especially if we engage in behaviors that manifest internalized supremacy.

Pause and Ponder

Pause and ponder the following questions considering what you've read.

- How do the seven Buddhist rights manifest in your current practice?
- What does authenticity look like when you encounter external opposition?
- How do you cultivate self-awareness in your practice?

DECONSTRUCTING AUTHENTICITY

Self-reflection requires us to confront and dismantle deeply ingrained beliefs, biases, and language patterns that we may not be fully aware of. This process demands vulnerability and honesty, which can be uncomfortable. It asks us to acknowledge the ways in which our perspectives, behaviors, and language have been shaped by systemic power dynamics. To truly connect with our authenticity and identity, we must be willing to question these internalized norms and engage in a continuous process of self-examination and growth. This connection to authenticity is essential because it allows us to interact with others from a place of genuine understanding and empathy and to foster more inclusive and equitable environments. By challenging our internalized supremacy and striving for authenticity, we can better align our actions and language with our values and contribute to positive change both personally and professionally.

Language is centrally tied up with identity, not just because language is how we construct our social identities but also because language is how we make sense of and codify our experience of the world. Language allows us to tell stories and narratives that position our selves in the world (McCarthy & Carter, 1994). Personal identities are shaped through unconscious activities that are framed by language usage (Fecho & Botzakis, 2007; Taubman, 2012). According to scholar Mikhail Bakhtin (1990), dialogue is the relationship between oneself and another individual. *Dialogical relationships* refer to the ways in which language usage and constructs between individuals or between individuals and systems can influence our understanding of self. The internal voices that create self, the various ideologies within self, and various other messages we consume via social media, movies, the news, and so on that portray a different ideology all have different discourses that impact how a person operates. In other words, societal context matters as a person is situated within many ideological communities, each having a different language to articulate values (Gee, 2015; van Loon, 2017).

Language is also reflective of the internal and external identities we adhere to. We define *external and internal identities* as concepts or relationships that influence our perception of self. Our internal and external identities are linked and respond to one another. For example, external identities might be constructed in relation to your spouse, nature around you, your school leader, and so on. Internal identities might be socialized beliefs around particular identity constructs (such as motherhood). For example, there can be dialogue between your students (external identity) and yourself (internal identity). The conversation with students is an external manifestation of internal beliefs. Depending on one's level of comfort, self-awareness, and understanding of authenticity, this dialogue can provide insight into the teacher while simultaneously making connections to students. As teachers, we can present a certain persona, but this might not align with the internal identities we hold and aspire to.

Navigating this tension is how we can learn to be more authentic.

As another example, let's consider my (Reshma's) internal and external identities as a woman and mother. I believe in equal distribution of responsibilities between myself and my spouse. I enjoy working as a source of financial autonomy and independence. However, there are many days when I have inner dialogues around how I see myself as a mother in light of my identity as a professional. These dialogues are wracked with guilt and self-criticism about my impact. Yet, I present a persona of handling my many responsibilities with ease. In fact, many of my female peers often say, "I don't know how you do it all."

Different identities can also respond to one another. Continuing with the previous example, my identity as a mother could impact my position as a consultant because I have less time with my children. This spawns an internal dialogue; I feel bad because

I'm not spending enough time with my kids. There can be external dialogue as well. Take a different example: a teacher's internal position of mother comes into dialogue with her principal when requesting not to work after school with students.

We define the concept of *dialogue* as a form of discourse—written and verbal transmission of information that reflects beliefs and understandings. Awareness of our constantly negotiating identities, as well as others' identities, is important in being authentic. No person is representative of one identity marker. The ways in which we see ourselves, how we want to show up in the classroom, the way others perceive us— these prompt internal and external dialogues that give clues about our authenticity.

Dialogical relationships, which are the interactions between two people, are not limited to internal mental processes or external verbal communication. Instead, they can be embodied, spatialized, and temporalized, reflecting the culture and power of multiple identities (Oleś, Brinthaupt, Dier, & Polak, 2020; van Loon, 2017). Language involves discourse explicitly or implicitly expressing socialized and ideological beliefs. Oppressive ideologies, in particular, are transmitted across generations through educational practices and socioeconomic experiences (Barthes, 2012; Storey, 2006). Teachers often replicate their inherent understanding of "good" pedagogy, rather than creating something entirely original (Akkerman & Meijer, 2011; Britzman, 2003). Bob Fecho and Stergios Botzakis (2007) assert that dialogic educators allow for the following.

- Raising questions and authoring responses by all participants fosters an inclusive environment where everyone's voice is valued, promoting deeper engagement and understanding.

- Embracing the importance of context and the non-neutrality of language highlights the influence of cultural and societal factors on communication and learning, encouraging critical awareness.

- Encouraging multiple perspectives broadens the scope of discussion and understanding, fostering a more comprehensive and empathetic view of complex issues.

- Flattening or disturbing existing hierarchies challenges traditional power structures, promoting equity and collaborative learning.

- Agreeing that learning is under construction and evolving emphasizes the dynamic nature of knowledge, encouraging continuous inquiry and adaptability.

Educators are human beings who bring complex internal and external identities with them to the classroom. As teachers, we must consider the ways in which our internal and external identities shape our understanding of teaching and learning. Within each of us, there exists a complex internal dialogue that speaks to our internal identity. This dialogue comprises our thoughts, beliefs, values, memories, and emotions. It's the ongoing conversation we have with ourselves, shaped by our personal experiences, upbringing, cultural background, and individual perspectives. This internal dialogue informs our identity, guiding our decisions, actions, and reactions. Figure 1.1 offers a series of activities educators can undertake within a collaborative team to consider the relationship between their internal and external identities.

Activity	Suggested Steps
Case study: Each week, team members present a series of students or scenarios that are directly related to interpersonal relationships between teachers and students. Team members take a solutions-oriented approach to unpacking the root of the concern.	Identify a student using a preconstructed set of criteria (for example, behavioral infractions, work completion, and so on). Discuss possible interventions that do not place blame on the student but rather focus on the relationship between the teacher and the student. Invite the student to the meeting to share their perspective and concerns. Offer suggestions and feedback for addressing the issue with clear measures for determining impact.
Focused intervisitation: Focused intervisitations are structured to be similar to typical intervisitations, but with a narrow emphasis. Specifically, a focused intervisitation would highlight the ways in which a teacher is authentically engaging with students.	Determine the logistics for the intervisitation. Establish a focus or guiding question for the intervisitation. The focus should be based on authenticity and language usage. For example: "During this intervisitation, I want to ensure that my students demonstrate that they feel safe in my classroom." Set clear measures for determining the teacher's impact based on the focus. For example: Monitor the number of students who are "on task." Study the language being used. Study students' body language and affect. Record the visit with a specific lens in mind. Debrief and reflect on the experience.

Figure 1.1: Navigating internal and external identities. *continued* →

Activity	Suggested Steps
Reflective dialogue journal: The reflective dialogue journal aims to help educators become more aware of their internal and external dialogue, uncover biases, and develop more inclusive communication practices. The journal can be shared between the teacher in question, students, and colleagues.	Create structured prompts: Each entry in the journal begins with a set of structured prompts designed to guide reflection. Prompts can focus on recent classroom interactions, language use, and personal reactions to diverse situations. Example prompts include the following. • Peer feedback: Periodically, teachers can share selected journal entries with a trusted colleague or mentor, as well as students, to gain insights and constructive feedback. This external perspective helps in identifying blind spots and developing strategies for improvement. • Action plans: Based on reflections and feedback, teachers create action plans to address areas for growth. These plans include specific, measurable goals for improving their internal and external dialogue.

*Visit **go.SolutionTree.com/diversityandequity** for a free reproducible version of this figure.*

Pause and Ponder

Pause and ponder the following questions considering what you've read.

- What are your internal identities?
- What are your external identities?
- What does it mean to be an authentic educator in light of your dialogic self?

Figure 1.2 (page 17) illustrates how as people we are constantly navigating our dialogical space influenced by the outside culture. We are constantly navigating our internal dialogues, our external dialogues, and our larger cultural influences.

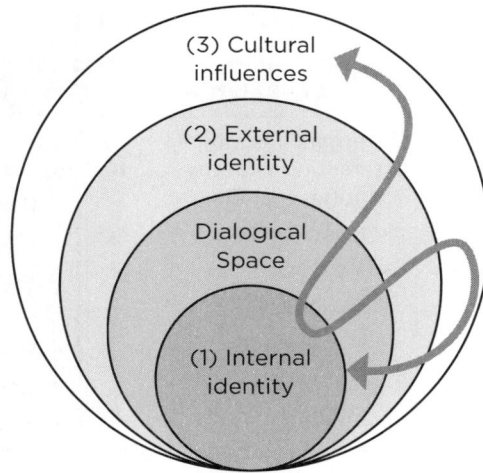

Figure 1.2: The relationship between external and internal identities.

The idea that we are constantly navigating our dialogical space, influenced by both internal and external identities, is a profound recognition of the complex nature of human identity and interaction. Our internal and external identities are not isolated; they are embedded within larger cultural influences. Culture encompasses shared values, norms, traditions, and worldviews that shape the way we perceive the world and interact with others. These cultural influences can be national, regional, ethnic, or even subcultural. They impact our language, communication styles, social norms, and expectations. *These dialogues are dynamic and ever evolving.* Our internal dialogues can change over time as we learn, grow, and adapt to new experiences. Similarly, our external dialogues are influenced by the context and the people we engage with. Cultural influences also evolve, reflecting shifts in society, politics, and global events.

Navigating these dialogical spaces is central to forming our identities and being authentic. Authenticity involves aligning our internal dialogues with our external expressions while respecting the cultural influences that shape us. Achieving this alignment is an ongoing process of self-discovery and self-expression. Table 1.1 (page 18) names examples of each of the internal and external identities named in figure 1.2.

In the case of Ms. Xenos from the introductory vignette, her internal identities didn't resonate with the cultural influences of her boss and the school's expectation that she utilize strategies from *Teach Like a Champion* by Doug Lemov (2010). Her internal self as a Harry Potter fanatic and as a person who thrives on creativity put her in opposition with the external position and expectations of her boss— particularly as they related to classroom management. The outcomes weren't good for her or for her students.

Table 1.1: Examples of Dialogical Components

(3) Cultural	(2) External	(1) Internal
Outside cultural components interacting with my identities include: • Policies • Systems • Positional dominance • Ideologies	External components interacting with my identities include: • My coworkers • My boss • My students • My parents • My partner • My best friend • My instructional coach	Internal components of my identities include: • Buddhist • Mother • World traveler • Reader • Relaxed • Chef • News junkie

To unpack this in working with Ms. Xenos, we asked, "What are the conditions that Ms. Xenos needs to feel more successful and bring her awareness of her internal self into her teaching?" We then discussed the potential risks and benefits in light of external influences and the larger outside culture to experiment in ways that may be outside of the *Teach Like a Champion* (Lemov, 2010) taxonomies but truer to her knowledge of herself and her knowledge of her students. This does not discount the impact of using technical approaches to classroom management such as the taxonomies. However, without knowing one's internal identity, the approaches will feel forced or fall flat.

Figure 1.3 shows an overview of Ms. Xenos's reflection on these themes.

What conditions do you need to be your authentic self?	What are the risks?	What are the benefits?
• More connection with students • License to experiment with things outside of the Lemov (2010) taxonomies without fear of retribution • Time to plan and time to implement lessons according to my preference	• Getting in trouble with administration • Failing • Being vulnerable with students and them rejecting it or me	• More job satisfaction • Feeling more successful • Feeling more excited • The ability to be more creative • Better meeting the needs of students

Figure 1.3: Sample teacher reflection on dialogical components.
*Visit **go.SolutionTree.com/diversityandequity** for a free reproducible version of this figure.*

As you can see from figure 1.3 (page 18), Ms. Xenos was able to articulate the conditions she needed to feel authentic. It was important to name as well as attend to the risks and benefits for cultivating an authentic pedagogical identity. Ms. Xenos was a newer teacher, and Jacobē did not want her to be diametrically opposed to her supervisor. This could have resulted in her being terminated. Therefore, Jacobē leveraged Ms. Xenos's reflections to address strategies within her locus of control. One such strategy was a cogenerative dialogue.

Cogenerative dialogue is a strategy developed by Christopher Emdin (2016) that prompts students to provide their teachers with feedback—ultimately minimizing the power hierarchy in classrooms and encouraging students to become owners of their learning experiences. When we asked students through cogenerative dialogues what they wanted more of in class, students asked for more interesting content, more one-to-one help to ensure understanding of the content, more time to collaborate with their peers in their work, and more opportunities to feel a connection with Ms. Xenos. We took student requests and added them to Ms. Xenos's self-reflection to plan changes for her classroom.

In our subsequent coaching conversations, Ms. Xenos decided on the following next steps.

- I will change my tone and cadence for emphasis and enthusiasm throughout the lesson during instances that feel right to me.
- I will try other facilitation methods (such as having students discuss with one another using small-group discussion protocols).
- I will switch out some of my texts based on student feedback while being mindful of standards and question types aligned to the original scripted curriculum.

Once Ms. Xenos understood that having a clear rationale for these changes would make it possible to communicate her plan to administration, she felt comfortable with a more authentic approach. She was able to move toward what was in line with her inner self considering her external factors because another external factor (Jacobē) was in her support system. Through this dialogical space she took risks that would potentially be better for her and her students, thus pushing against the grain of the outer culture. Ms. Xenos's example shows the complex nature of authenticity and how our personal identities interact with external positions and the outside culture in a way that requires us to continuously navigate our degree of authenticity. As education faces unprecedented challenges—such as stagnant wages, restrictive policies, and heightened political scrutiny—the urgency of supporting teacher authenticity becomes clearer. Authenticity helps mitigate the negative effects of these pressures by enabling teachers to feel genuine in their roles, fostering a sense of purpose and resilience (Kraft & Lyon, 2024).

The relationship between authenticity and a teacher's impact is deeply intertwined with the profession's broader struggles and aspirations. Historically, authenticity in teaching has fostered genuine connections with students, creating a more engaging and resilient classroom culture. When teachers feel free to be authentic, their confidence and job satisfaction often increase, inspiring students to participate more fully. Education's steep decline in status, influenced by factors such as stagnant wages, restrictive policies, and increased political scrutiny, threaten this essential authenticity. The profession experienced similar declines in the 1970s before reform efforts in the 1980s, including support for professional autonomy and increased resources, revived its standing. The challenges and changes that teachers face today—exacerbated by increased stress, perceived losses of authority, and burdensome policies—highlight the critical need to nurture an environment where teachers can teach authentically. Authenticity not only increases a teacher's personal satisfaction but also directly affects their long-term influence on students, enhancing educational quality and addressing attrition issues. Recognizing and bolstering this authenticity, through support for autonomy and community-driven reforms, holds promise for reelevating the teaching profession and ultimately sustaining a high-quality education system for future generations (Kraft & Lyon, 2024).

Thus, there is a substantive amount of overlap between our personal identities and our teacher identities, although the external positions may try to suppress it. Hiding our internal identities or failing to authentically show up creates circumstances where teacher identities feel forced, thereby creating challenges and even conflict for the teacher and students. Issues such as inauthentic lesson implementations and fragile relationships between teachers and students can perpetuate inequities in the classroom. Therefore, we pushed Ms. Xenos to reflect on her inner self, examine the risks and benefits of being her authentic self, and lean into what felt true to her, as well as realistically feasible, based on her reflection to disrupt the inequities occurring in her classroom. Being authentic in the classroom directly enhances a teacher's effectiveness. When teachers bring their true selves to their work, students sense sincerity and are more likely to engage deeply, trust more readily, and participate actively in learning. Authenticity also boosts a teacher's confidence, fueling enthusiasm and commitment. Teachers who feel genuine in their roles show increased job satisfaction and resilience, qualities linked to better student outcomes and lower teacher burnout. This connection between authenticity and teaching quality is undeniable; an authentic teacher is not only a happier teacher but also a more impactful one.

Where do you find external and internal tension in your work as an educator? Use the reproducible "Reflecting on External and Internal Identities" (page 23) to write about the conditions you need to be your authentic self.

If you have started the first step of reflecting on the tensions that impact your internal or inner self, great! Your brain is primed and ready for our continued conversations around positions, identity, and culture. We cannot begin to think about the tensions we experience as practitioners without attending to the role of intersectionality, culture, and cultural competence. We will delve into these three concepts in chapter 2 (page 25).

Pause and Ponder

Pause and ponder the following questions considering what you've read.

- How would you describe the relationship between your external and internal identities?
- What factors might pose a risk to your perception of authenticity?
- How would you address potential risks based on your locus of control?

PURSUING AUTHENTICITY

Teacher authenticity, when grounded in a solid identity, contributes to a positive learning environment by establishing trust, creating a sense of belonging, and encouraging open communication. Authentic teachers bring sincerity and transparency into their interactions, which fosters a supportive atmosphere where students feel comfortable expressing themselves and engaging in the learning process. Teacher authenticity positively impacts student engagement and academic success by promoting a healthy teacher-student relationship. When students perceive their teachers as authentic and relatable, they are more likely to actively participate in class, seek guidance when needed, and feel motivated to succeed academically. Authenticity contributes to a positive classroom culture that nurtures student growth and achievement.

Through reflecting on our inner self and looking toward authenticity, we aspire for classrooms and schools that:

- Engage in student-centered education practices that are rooted in liberation and not marginalization

- Lean into self-introspection and personal growth so we don't harm others

- Have strong teacher-student relationships that foster a safe, inclusive, and welcoming learning environment where teachers and students alike can be vulnerable and take risks

- Are built on a common trust between students and teachers, knowing that when teachers are authentic, students are more likely to trust their intentions, thus leading to a more positive, joyful environment

- Promote critical thinking by encouraging both teachers and students to share in ways that are grounded in respect so that students feel safe to take intellectual risks

- Encourage innovation and dreaming for students and teachers

- Stand on collective healing from past educational traumas

We envision a future of schooling that is student centered, inclusive, and liberatory. Where are you on this journey? Not here yet? That's OK. Stay on this journey with us as we move toward authenticity. By valuing and promoting authenticity in teaching, we can create a more effective and meaningful educational experience that benefits both students and educators.

SUMMING UP

The act of being an authentic educator requires us to reflect on who we are as people, first, and how our identities manifest in practice. As you unearth the elements that make you who you are, you will see a shift in your classroom paradigm. Students will humanize you because you are presenting elements of your personality that are the foundation for building substantive rapport with the young people in your charge.

Consider the following key takeaways from this chapter.

- Authenticity requires us to think about our lived experiences and the ways in which we have been coached to exhibit these attributes as well as hide them.

- We need to name the conditions under which we can be our most authentic self. If those conditions do not exist, we might need to make them.

- Centering authenticity allows us to seek liberation for teachers and students alike.

Reflecting on External and Internal Identities

In the space provided in the chart, write a short summary of your current situation. Then, take time to read and respond to the prompts, reflecting on the conditions you need to be your authentic self as well as the risks and benefits involved in pursuing these conditions.

Your situation:

What conditions do you need to be your authentic self?

What are the risks?

What are the benefits?

Journaling for Further Reflection

In the space provided, journal your responses to the following prompts.

How do you define the idea of authenticity? What parallels or differences do you have in relation to the content of this chapter?

How would your students define the idea of authenticity? How might you reconcile your definition of authenticity with their perceptions?

Where are you on your journey toward authenticity? What hinders you?

CHAPTER 2

TEACHER IDENTITY, INTERSECTIONALITY, AND CULTURAL COMPETENCE

Aja has been teaching ELA at the same school for the past five years. I, Reshma, had the privilege of coaching her from her second year of teaching. Right away, I realized there was something unique about Aja, especially when she was in the same room with her co-teacher. Her eighth graders responded to her requests, could be seen coming to her during lunch just to talk, and consistently bought into the content she taught. Her students loved her lessons so much they even created alternate theories about the characters' lives. They speculated whether Walter was the father of Ruth's baby in *A Raisin in the Sun* (Hansberry, 1994). "Miss, Walter's always at the bar! How is it that she is pregnant? It's a phantom baby to get his attention."

Why do students respond to her in this way? What is it about Aja and other teachers like her that prompts students to gravitate to them? They know themselves and are comfortable with students seeing their realness. While conducting research for this book, I, Reshma, once asked her what she believes allows her to have a substantive relationship with her students. She said, "Some of them [teachers] are always telling me not to tell the kids what is happening in my life. But why shouldn't I? Telling them would put me at ease, which then puts them at ease." Aja, within appropriate constructs, shares her life experiences to empathize and connect with students. These habits come naturally to her as a result of her own socialization and cultural frame of reference.

In this chapter, we build on the concept of authenticity that we introduced in chapter 1 (page 9) by exploring the role of identity. We will examine why identity, intersectionality, and cultural competence are essential for teachers to show up authentically for students. We will begin by briefly discussing the idea of socialization. Socialization is crucial to our understanding of identity, intersectionality, and cultural competence. We, as teachers, are not blank slates. We are molded by those who have loved and cared for us and the institutions we frequent. Let's take a look!

UNDERSTANDING THE CYCLE OF SOCIALIZATION

Social conditioning and systems shape each person's worldview, thoughts, and actions. Sociologist Bobbie Harro's (2000) Cycle of Socialization offers a framework for understanding this phenomenon (figure 2.1).

Stage	Description	Key Points
Beginning	Birth into a world with existing systems of oppression.	No consciousness, choice, blame, or guilt. Lack of information about social identity and power.
First Socialization	Socialized by loved ones.	Taught roles, rules, self-concepts, and expectations. Shaped dreams, values, and future.
Institutional and Cultural Socialization	Exposed to messages about power and who should have it.	Bombarded by institutions like education, religion, law, and so on. Internalization of biases and stereotypes.
Enforcements	System of rewards and punishments.	Keeps us playing by the rules. Those who don't are sanctioned or victimized.
Results	Negative outcomes for those with and without power.	Misperceptions, dissonance, silence, stress, collusion, inequality, anger, guilt, hate, self-destructive behaviors, violence, and crime.

Stage	Description	Key Points
The Continuation	Choice to maintain the status quo.	Failure to challenge or question the system.
Direction for Change	Movement toward liberation.	Begin to think, challenge, and question the system. See the problem with the picture.
The Core Factors that keep us in the cycle include ignorance, insecurity, confusion, obliviousness, and fear.		

Source: Adapted from Harro, 2000.

Figure 2.1: Harro's cycle of socialization.

Harro (2000) specializes in thinking about the ways in which we are conditioned to see the world through our social interactions. When we see oppression, many of us wonder why we can't just get along despite the many differences resulting from our diverse identities. Harro explains that it's just not that simple:

> We are each born into a specific set of *social identities*, related to [gender, ethnicity, skin color, first language, age, ability status, religion, sexual orientation, and economic class], and these social identities predispose us to unequal *roles* in the dynamic system of oppression. We are then socialized by powerful sources in our worlds to play the roles prescribed by an inequitable social system. (p. 15)

Teachers enter schooling spaces, of their own choosing, and enact their lived socialization, thereby continuing systems of inequity that harm our most marginalized groups. For example, if we consider seemingly harmless statements that characterize White people and schools as safer, better, and good, what we are really seeing is the socialized practices that have resulted in teachers leaning into Whiteness as the pinnacle. Author and policy advocate Heather C. McGhee (2021) writes about socialization in her book *The Sum of Us*:

> The truth is, children do learn to categorize, and rank, people by race while they are still toddlers. By age three or four, white children and children of color have absorbed the message that white is better and both are likely to select white playmates if given a choice. (p. 184)

Harro (2000) argues that there are several layers of socialization that we encounter. When we are born, we enter a world marked by systems of oppression and marginalization. As newborns, we do not have access to this information, but rather first experience socialization through our caregivers and the beliefs, identities, and ideologies they hold. Then, we ultimately become a part of institutions where we engage in cultural socialization. Culture, which we explore later in this chapter, has several different meanings. These cultural ideas become a part of our psyche and development of self. Our life experiences reinforce and perpetuate socialization unless we take the time to disconnect and reflect on the institutions that have buoyed our development. Once we begin to reflect and challenge oppressive ideologies, we can then forge a path of liberation and authenticity.

Throughout this chapter, we ask you to think about the variables that have influenced your identity. We juxtapose this concept with intersectionality and the premise of cultural competence. For us to become more authentic in our practice and behaviors, we have to consider the ways in which we were socialized.

THINKING ABOUT IDENTITY

Writer and civil rights activist James Baldwin (1963) writes in *The Fire Next Time*, "There are too many things we do not wish to know about ourselves" (p. 72). The antidote to this willful ignorance? Love. As Baldwin (1963) writes:

> Love takes off the masks that we fear we cannot live without and know we cannot live within. I use the word love here not merely in the personal sense but as a state of being, or a state of grace—not in the infantile American sense of being made happy but in the tough and universal sense of quest and daring and growth. (p. 78)

At the start of this chapter, we met Aja. A decade later, Aja—now a ten-year veteran teacher—continues to manifest elements of her identity that allow her to connect with students. In reflecting on her socialization, there are communal experiences that she can draw from in order to establish a connection with her students. If you might not share common experiences with your students, then know this is OK! Leaning into authenticity requires us to acknowledge this potential gap in the first place! Don't force a connection. Instead, take the time to build relationships. In this chapter, we continue to explore the notion of authenticity but in relation to identity, cultural competence, and intersectionality and how you might use these ideas to cultivate strong connections to your students. Let's begin by defining identity.

Identity is a multifaceted and dynamic concept that encompasses the totality of who a person is, shaped by various factors such as culture, ethnicity, gender, socioeconomic status, and personal experiences. It is the amalgamation of both visible and invisible attributes that influence how individuals perceive themselves and are perceived by others (Darling-Hammond, 1998). Identity formation is contextual and the result of a symbiotic relationship—particularly within schooling settings (Flum & Kaplan, 2012). Awareness of identity is crucial for a teacher's authenticity because it involves recognizing and understanding one's own beliefs, biases, and cultural background. Authenticity in teaching stems from genuine self-awareness, allowing educators to bring their true selves into the classroom. When teachers are aware of their own identity, they can navigate interactions with students more genuinely, fostering trust and connection.

This happens over time as we reflect on how we see ourselves and how others see us. We are not advocating for wanting to morph to the desires of others. Rather it is an open conversation with ourselves and constituents. If the act of reflection can feel hard, begin with two tangible steps: record your conversations or practice, and use the dialogue journal in the reproducible "Reflecting on External and Internal Identities" (page 23).

In essence, the awareness and understanding of one's identity are fundamental aspects of effective teaching, contributing to teacher authenticity, cultural competence, and ultimately fostering meaningful connections with students.

Pause and Ponder

Pause and ponder the following questions considering what you've read.

- Make a mental list of three identity markers you use to describe yourself. How have these developed over time?
- Think of the person closest to you and whose opinion you trust most. How would they describe your identity?
- What benefits have your identities afforded you? In what ways have your identities been marginalized?

CONSIDERING INTERSECTIONALITY

Intersectionality didn't begin as the more holistic concept of identity many of us know today. Given that, it's helpful to understand its origins, which begin with legal scholar and civil rights advocate Kimberlé Crenshaw, who developed the concept of intersectionality in 1989 to address the erasure of Black women from legal scenarios or circumstances. Crenshaw's (1991) seminal work posits that Black women often are not seen for the multifaceted elements of their identity. Through a series of legal case studies, she argues:

> Black women can experience discrimination in ways that are both
> similar to and different from those experienced by white women
> and Black men. Black women sometimes experience discrimina-
> tion in ways similar to white women's experiences; sometimes
> they share very similar experiences with Black men. Yet often they
> experience double-discrimination—the combined effects of prac-
> tices which discriminate on the basis of race, and on the basis
> of sex. . . . Black women's experiences are much broader than
> the general categories that discrimination discourse provides. Yet
> the continued insistence that Black women's demands and needs
> be filtered through categorical analyses that completely obscure
> their experiences guarantees their needs will seldom be addressed.
> (Crenshaw, 1989, pp. 149–150)

Black women are only afforded protections if they are recognized by larger systems
or structures that would protect those rights among other populations (such as White
men or women). However, Black women are rarely seen for the totality of their identity and the connections between all elements of their identity, which include but
are not limited to race, sex, gender, class, physical ability, and neurodiversity—and
the list goes on.

Intersectionality arose as a desire to question and challenge White Eurocentric norms
around what it means to be a woman and how this construct is challenged when we
consider the other variables of identity. In the decades since Crenshaw's (1991) work on
intersectionality began, the term has extended beyond Black women to encompass people holding other marginalized identities, providing a framework to understand how a
person's multiple and unique identities contribute to their full self and their experience
in the world. Writer and speaker Ijeoma Oluo (2018) defines *intersectionality* as "the
belief that our social justice movements must consider all of the intersections of identity, privilege and oppression that people face in order to be just and effective" (p. 74).

In the years since Crenshaw's (1991) publication, constructs of identity have
become more nuanced in large part due to the evolution of larger identity markers.
For example, at the time of her publication, the larger gender identity narrative centered on a binary—male or female. As of this writing, the understanding of gender
has evolved to recognize people who identify as male, female, transgender, gender
neutral, nonbinary, genderqueer, and many more (Gold, 2018)! For the purpose
of intersectionality, the inclusion of such nuanced constructs can result in complex
identities. Yet, the premise behind Crenshaw's understanding of intersectionality
remains the same. It means that we can move away from dividing people into categories and begin to see them as whole humans in all their complexity.

Table 2.1 offers examples of how larger identity categories have given way to more
nuanced identities.

Table 2.1: Nuanced Understandings of Intersectionality

Initial Category	Nuanced Understandings
Race	• Multiracial identities • Socially constructed racial paradigms • Reclaimed racial identities (such as Black and Latinx) • Ethnicity and culture • Nationality and associated racial designation
Gender	• Gender assigned at birth • Self-selected gender identity • Social construct of identity • Sexual identity in relation to gender identity • Sexual orientation and associated identity • LGBTQIA+ self-identification
Class	• Social contexts • Schooling experiences • Upper, middle, and lower social classes • Upper, middle, and lower economic classes • Friendship circles • Accessibility to people in power and privilege due to parental access and the preceding concepts
Ability	• Physical limitations or modifications • Cognitive needs • Neurodiversity • Mental illness and health • Language accessibility

Intersectionality asks us as teachers to recognize that we are the sum of our parts and calls us to reflect on the identities we hold and how they are interconnected. A whole person encompasses all their identities and how they interact. One cannot divorce certain elements of identity and remain their full self. This means identity categories are not static but dynamic, shaped by the influences of our multiple identities and our lived experience.

For example, Reshma grew up in an Indo-Caribbean household. Traditional beliefs pertaining to female behaviors were instilled within her through explicit and implicit interactions with her parents (some examples include sitting with legs together, helping with household chores, being seen and not heard in public spaces, and taking care of younger siblings). Being the older female sibling also brought with it an additional layer of complexity, specifically as it related to setting a good example or forging a path for others. These practices were ingrained in her psyche and had an impact on her behavior for many years.

Alongside these traditional beliefs, Reshma developed unlikely knowledge and skills from her father, who was an auto mechanic. He would often say, "What need do I have for sons when I have daughters like y'all?" He taught Reshma how to change her oil, understand how a car engine functioned, measure tire tread depth, and more. She constantly surprises service writers at car dealerships with this knowledge. Reshma's identity as a female is linked to her upbringing, but her nuanced lived experiences influence her perceptions of what exactly this means for her own identity. The ability to move between spaces based on the identities she holds is a perfect example of intersectionality. She does not remove one element of self while in a space that requires a different presence. Rather, her internal dialogue (chapter 1, page 13) marries all of her identities together. As an educator, she uses this same methodology when determining how to show up for the students and teachers she supports.

As educators become aware of their unique identity and how they desire to manifest it within their teacher persona, they begin to appreciate the need for cultural competence. It empowers and informs their work in disrupting inequities in their life and their classroom.

EMBRACING CULTURAL COMPETENCE

Cultural competence is the capacity of the individual to embed and honor the subtleties associated with cultural monikers colleagues, peers, or students might subscribe to. Teachers who appreciate these attributes in themselves experience greater ease and sense of self; they bring this cultural appreciation into the classroom, too, embracing the complexity of their students.

Unpacking one's identity requires navigating the implicit and explicit modes of cultural competence. We cannot discuss identity without thinking about our relationship to cultural competence. Cultural competence involves the ability to understand, appreciate, and effectively interact with people from diverse cultural backgrounds while acknowledging our perceptions of those people. Teacher awareness of identity, including owning one's unique cultural background, is a prerequisite for cultural competence. It allows educators to approach diversity with sensitivity, acknowledging and respecting the varied identities within their classroom. Knowing oneself is a transformative process that enables teachers to authentically connect with their students. When educators have a deep understanding of their own identity, values, and biases, they are better equipped to relate to the diverse identities present in their classrooms. This self-awareness fosters empathy, facilitates open communication, and creates a learning environment where students feel seen, heard, and valued.

No journey relating to self, identity, and culture is ever complete. The journey is ever winding. We never arrive at a destination—we only uncover various layers of ourselves as we molt. We come to new realizations and awareness as we make connections between our internal and external positions as well as associated tensions. Therefore, we want to emphasize that the "competence" is a misnomer. No one is ever truly competent when it comes to culture because there is so much *we do not know*. The concept of cultural competence, with its emphasis on understanding and appreciating diverse cultures, requires a posture of curiosity rather than judgment. This shift in perspective requires adopting an asset-oriented approach rather than a deficit-oriented one. The asset-based posture of curiosity encourages active engagement and continuous learning. It invites questions, conversations, and a willingness to step outside one's comfort zone. When we let curiosity take the lead, we seek out diverse voices, experiences, and narratives to broaden our understanding. On the other hand, a deficit-oriented approach puts our focus on what is lacking or perceived as "different" from our own cultural norms. This mindset can lead to stereotypes, biases, and a failure to appreciate the inherent strengths within each culture. Embracing a posture of curiosity means approaching different cultures with an open mind and a genuine desire to understand. It involves acknowledging that each culture brings unique strengths, values, and perspectives to the table. Instead of viewing differences as deficits, this approach recognizes them as valuable assets that contribute to the richness of our collective human experience.

An asset-oriented perspective allows teachers to see cultural diversity as a source of strength and resilience. It recognizes the wealth of knowledge, skills, and perspectives that individuals from different cultures bring to any given context. By adopting this approach, teachers not only challenge stereotypes but also create an environment that celebrates the unique assets that each cultural group contributes. Embracing curiosity and asset orientation enhances educators' cultural competence. It allows them to engage in meaningful and respectful interactions with individuals from diverse backgrounds, thereby leaning into authentic interactions (Mayfield, 2020). Teachers' ability to navigate cultural differences is greatly strengthened when they approach each encounter with a genuine curiosity about the richness of diverse experiences and an acknowledgment of the assets inherent in every culture. Fostering a posture of curiosity and adopting an asset-oriented perspective is not just a mindset shift; it's a transformative approach to cultural competence. It opens doors to authentic connections, dispels stereotypes, and enriches our understanding of the diverse world we inhabit.

Scholars define culture in a variety of ways. Generally speaking, *culture* can refer to the social contexts, interactions, and encounters that inform how individuals might make meaning of the world around them in relation to themselves. This cognitive construct often carries with it various language or speech patterns that subsequently influence a person's view of themselves and of the world. Sound a little bit like intersectionality? The two concepts are interrelated.

In the context of this book, we think about culture in two notable categories: *big*-C *Culture* and *little*-c *culture* (Hammond, 2015a). Table 2.2 provides a brief overview of the difference between big-*C* Culture and little-*c* culture.

Table 2.2: Overview of Big-*C* Culture and Little-*c* culture

Examples of Big-*C* Culture	Examples of Little-*c* Culture
• Race or visible phenotypes • Gender identity • Age • Language • Visible neurodiversity	• Nonvisible interests or passions (such as skateboarding or roller derby) • Being an introvert versus an extrovert • Religious beliefs or ideologies • Nonvisible neurodiversity

Big-*C* Culture is more visible than little-*c* culture; we can visibly discern it without much probing or wondering. It is the branches and leaves shown in Zaretta Hammond's (2015a) culture tree, visible in figure 2.2. It refers to apparent qualities such as age or race, whereas if we begin to dig a bit deeper toward the roots, we observe a new layer of more obscure little-*c* cultural qualities, such as religion and values. For example, if someone presents with phenotypes associated with the Indian subcontinent, you might assume evidence of Indian ancestry. By probing below the surface or sincerely striving to understand the person in question, one might learn more about the individual's family beliefs, regional paradigms, variations on cultures, and so on.

We bring perceptions of others based on our lived experiences and, consequences of the cultures we are exposed to. While we might have commonalities based on our big-*C* cultures, there are still elements about ourselves and each other that remain unknown. We must spend time pulling back the layers. For more on this topic, read Vernita Mayfield's (2020) text, *Cultural Competence Now*, and complete the self-assessment tool that promotes reflection on areas of strength and opportunity as it relates to cultural competency.

Level	Description	Key Points
Surface Culture	Observable patterns and behaviors; low emotional impact on trust	Food, holidays, customs, drama, music, art, language, literature, stories, and so on
Shallow Culture	Unspoken rules and norms; high emotional impact on trust	Concepts of time, acceptable food sources, ways of handling emotion, personal space, eye contact, tempo of work, nonverbal communication, child-rearing principles, nature of relationships, theories of wellness and disease
Deep Culture	Collective unconscious beliefs, norms, and values; intense emotional impact on trust	Decision making, concepts of self, worldview, definitions of kinship and group identity, cosmology, spirituality and concept of a higher power, relationship to nature and animals, preferences for cooperation or competition, notion of fairness

Source: Adapted from Hammond, 2015a.

Figure 2.2: Hammond's levels of culture.

While the journey to cultural competency is not terminal, there is a spectrum by which we can evaluate our dispositions relating to culture and cultural practices. The spectrum, created by the Center for Culturally Proficient Educational Practice (n.d.), has been adapted for this context to represent the experiences of teachers in the classroom. There are six phases that teachers might want to be mindful of as they are progressing: (1) cultural destructiveness, (2) cultural incapacity, (3) cultural blindness, (4) cultural pre-competence, (5) cultural competence, and (6) cultural proficiency. Figure 2.3 (page 36) provides several examples of teacher behaviors as they relate to each component.

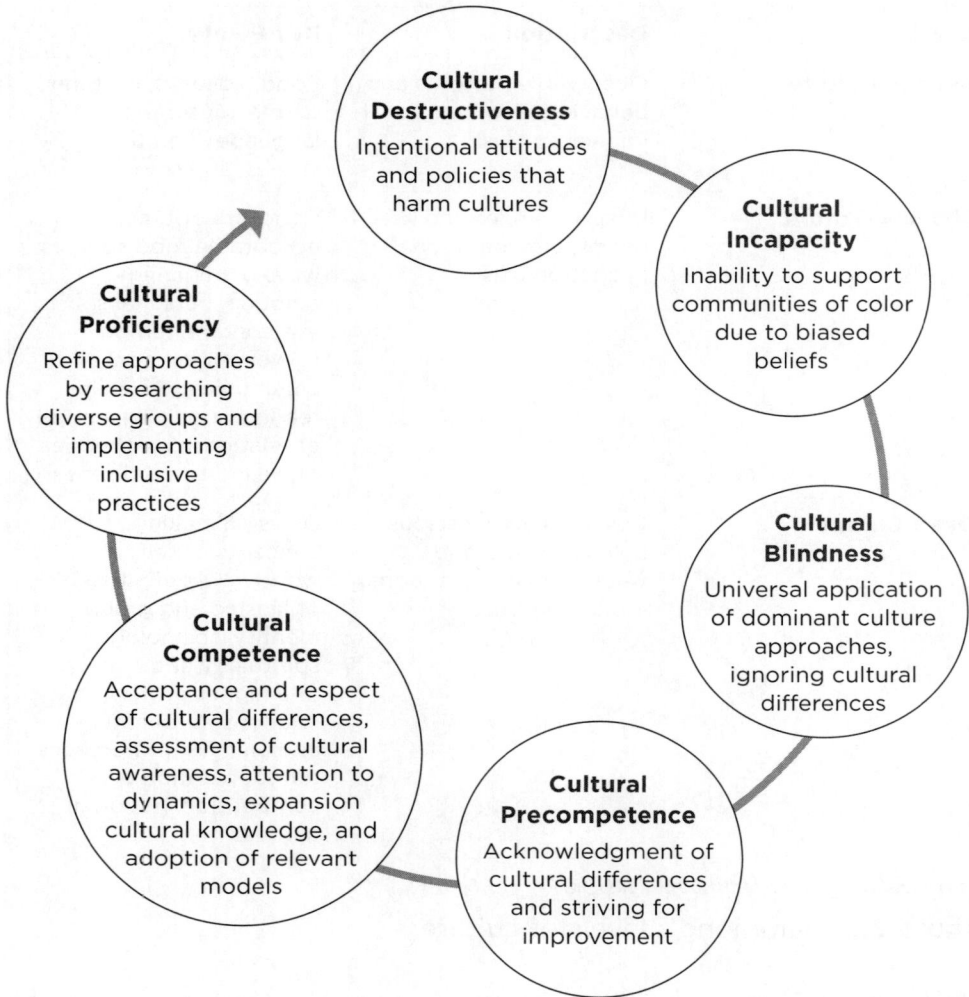

Source: Adapted from the Center for Culturally Proficient Educational Practice, n.d.

Figure 2.3: An overview of cultural competence based on a continuum.

As teachers reflect on their identities, they leverage this awareness to enact classroom practices that aspire to cultural competence. Engaging in cultural competence as a practitioner is a shift in disposition that manifests in tangible practices. This happens with time and practice as teachers intentionally reflect on their beliefs and understanding of cultural competence. This reflection prompts subtle shifts in practice. Table 2.3 offers two simple strategies for demonstrating cultural competence in the classroom while continuously working on one's understanding of the concept.

Table 2.3: Strategies for Demonstrating Cultural Competence

Domain	Definition	Dispositional Shifts	Tangible Shifts
Culturally Responsive Teaching Materials	The materials we place in front of students represent what we consider to be important information. Our beliefs and assumptions can often run in opposition to students' lived experiences, resulting in cultural blindness. Intentionally asking students what they seek to learn as well as what might be of interest to them opens up opportunities to include additional modes of thinking.	Pause to reflect on the content you're presenting to students. Check biases based on lived experiences and assumptions of students. Engage in research that furthers your learning and reflection (for example, listening to podcasts and reading alternative perspectives).	Integrate diverse and culturally relevant materials into the curriculum. Select textbooks, literature, and resources that represent a variety of cultures and perspectives. Highlight opinions and modes of thinking that are different from traditionally taught practices (for example, the oral tradition).
Incorporating Multicultural Perspectives	The educational system has inadvertently trained us to favor a specific mode of thinking or information source, contingent on the subject matter. Embracing multiple perspectives entails transcending the notion of a singular correct approach and delving into a spectrum of divergent viewpoints. This practice enables us to showcase cultural competence.	Create formal and informal opportunities for teachers to learn more about students' lives, beliefs, and origin stories. Conduct research into content you're teaching rather than simply repeating information. Cultivate an intentional drive to innovate content.	Teach subjects from multiple cultural perspectives, providing a well-rounded view of historical events, literature, and scientific discoveries. Encourage students to research and present on topics related to their cultural heritage. Conduct intellectual research on the origin of particular topics and present diverse perspectives (for example, the origin of zero, HeLa cells, and so on).

By now you might be wondering, "OK, so what?" Cultural competence is related to intersectionality because to appreciate others we must know ourselves first. If you think back to chapter 1 (page 9), you'll see that continuous reflection on identity is crucial to appreciating intersectionality, especially as we consider the external and internal tensions we might feel in various social contexts and how to disrupt inequities in our classrooms. Although this inner work can seem abstract at times, it is the crucial first step for teachers. We cannot offer to our students what we don't first possess ourselves. As teachers engage with their own identities, understand their intersectionality, and embrace their cultural expressions, they become more confident and self-aware. Confidence creates greater comfort, ease, and sincere relationships with students. Through such relationships, students become receptive to learning (Emdin, 2016; Stembridge, 2020).

Pause and Ponder

Pause and ponder the following questions considering what you've read.

- In three words, define cultural competence.
- How would you describe the difference between big-*C* Culture and little-*c* culture?
- In one sentence, name where you are on the cultural competence spectrum and why you think this is the case.

SEEING THE CONNECTION BETWEEN AUTHENTICITY AND TEACHER IDENTITY

While visiting another eighth-grade classroom, we observed a teacher discussing trauma-based substance abuse in Sherman Alexie's (2017) *The Absolutely True Diary of a Part-Time Indian*. Prior to students launching into a direct discussion about the topic, the teacher shared an anecdote with students about how the book connected to her. She said, "My dad was an alcoholic, and he sometimes switched his behaviors between mimicking Rowdy and Junior's dad." Students nodded in understanding, a few using nonverbal signals to indicate similar thinking or experiences. After sharing, she asked students to make connections between the text and their lives as well as discuss long-term implications for Junior's troubled home context. When we asked why she took this vulnerable approach, she shrugged and said, "There is always a risk, but my family and life have made me who I am. So, in a way, I connect to Junior and want students to find those connections, too."

Teachers, of course, should use discernment to ensure they're sharing appropriately with students. Knowing the intersections of your identity and sharing (appropriately) allows students to connect as they see themselves in your experiences.

We reiterate here the importance of authenticity to teacher identity and provide several reflective activities to continue the internal cultivation of these concepts. Figure 2.4 illustrates connections between authenticity and intersectionality.

Intersectionality	Classroom Presence	Teacher Identity
Intersectionality requires us to consider the various identities we hold, the ways in which they interact with each and the implications for power, privilege and oppression. In tandem to unpacking our intersectionality, we must also consider our understanding an appreciation for the cultures we belong to and the cultures of others.	Teaching is a personal practice, whether we want to admit it or not. Elements of our various intersections often manifest in the interactions we have with students and the ways we view the students themselves. Our presence is a manifestation of our sense of self as constructed based on the various identities.	Whether we want to admit it or not, there is a substantive amount of overlap with our personal identity and teacher identity. Hiding our true selves or failing to authentically show up in the classroom only creates circumstances where teacher identities feel forced. Lean into who you are and own it. Chance are, the students will appreciate you more as a result.

Figure 2.4: The relationship between authenticity and intersectionality.

As figure 2.4 explains, when we explicitly consider the intersection of our personalities, we become more comfortable in our skin. This comfort prompts a sense of psychological safety that allows us to create the desired presence and identity within a classroom. Teachers unconsciously emulate those educators in their lives who had a profound impact on their learning experiences (Ramkellawan-Arteaga, 2017). Inherent to this behavior is the belief that practicing these same pedagogical moves will make them as effective an educator as the "model teacher." This might be a successful strategy in some contexts, but the reality is that students, their interests, and their experiences are constantly evolving. Humans are designed to evolve; we are not meant to be static. Therefore, educators should be dynamic in their approaches as well.

Dynamism stems from the continuous reflection on our own identities and lived experiences. We've had many experiences through our coaching practice of learning something new about ourselves or discovering an innovative way to connect to students. We find ourselves saying, "Dang, if only we were in the classroom—that would be such a dope lesson." In other instances, we cringe from embarrassment as we recognize failures in past teaching moments and wish for a do-over. Regardless of where you find yourself in your journey, continue to pull back the layers to learn more about yourself. One way to achieve this is through student interviews.

"I just don't understand why they [students] aren't interested." If we had a dollar for every time we heard this statement! The antidote to this problem is simple: ask students for their opinion.

Students should have the opportunity to share their feedback and concerns about a teacher's performance without the filter of a survey. Surveys allow for ambiguity and perception-based processing of the results by the recipient. A live interview or focus group ensures that the teacher is directly hearing the feedback and asking follow-up questions in real-time circumstances.

The following are some key conditions required to make these student interviews successful.

- **Demonstrate trust, honesty, and transparency:** Create an environment of curiosity, openness, and nonjudgment. Students will not be honest and vulnerable if there's any chance they'll be judged, punished, or singled out. Ask yourself and answer honestly, "Will I hold it against a student if they say something that offends me or that I disagree with?" If the answer is yes, don't go any further. You're not ready. If the answer is no, you're ready to proceed. Name for students that you want them to be honest with you so that it will ensure you are growing as a person and becoming a better teacher. This helps to create a sense of trust that allows students to open up and share.

- **Select a wide range of students:** It might be tempting to pick the students who are vocal or whom you have a great relationship with. By all means, include them. However, also attend to students who are more reserved or with whom you've had a difficult relationship. These students are likely to provide the most honest feedback.

- **Plan your questions:** Have a minimum of five questions ready. Students will likely say things or make comments that make you want to ask follow-up questions. Please do! But don't go into the conversation blind. Here are a few sample questions relating to authenticity.

  - What do you wish you knew about me as a person?

  - How do you believe I can improve my practice as a teacher?

  - What suggestions do you have for improving my relationship with you and other students in the class?

  - Do you think I show my "realness" when teaching? Why or why not?

  - What feedback do you have for me about my teaching and how interesting you might find me and my instruction?

Keep the conversation to about ten to fifteen minutes. Teachers can determine the frequency with which they occur as well as the number of students who participate.

EXAMINING LAYERS OF TEACHER IDENTITY

How do teachers become more aware of their identity? One strategy is to conceptualize identity in layers. We can think about teacher identity in the following three layers.

1. **Aspirational identity:** This refers to idealized attributes new teachers aspire to manifest in their classroom—the image a new teacher has for who they want to be as an educator. This vision is based on the experiences we have as learners, our lives outside of schooling spaces, and the interactions we have with "model teachers," whether they be real or fictionalized.

2. **Reality-based identity:** The reality of our teaching practice is contingent on the context in which we choose to teach. In some instances, our aspirational identities as teachers become manifested because the context is in alignment. In other instances, we enter learning spaces that are markedly different from our own and need to rectify the reality of our context with the practices and capacities we bring to the space. For example, compare Aja and Ms. Xenos, whom you read about earlier in this chapter. Aja was able to embody her vision of herself as a teacher because the school context supported the development of these attributes. In contrast, Ms. Xenos's school community did not foster her self-described behaviors. Teachers often have to adapt in ways that reflect their school contexts and can ultimately diminish their authenticity.

3. **Manifested identity:** This is the intentional implementation and execution of a teacher identity that students interact with and experience daily. This manifestation can be a hybrid of the aspirational and reality, or it can be a completely revised entity depending on the teacher's reflection on their perception of self, culture, or intersections. The manifested identity should be one that students can connect to, that they recognize as authentic, and that helps to promote learning experiences.

The ways in which a teacher sees each of these layers impacts their ability to show up as their authentic self. Think back to intersectionality. We often have overlap of numerous identity markers. Intersectionality applies in this case as teachers pivot between the three layers of their pedagogical identity. Regardless of where teachers are in their tenure, they tend to pivot across these three domains when considering the type of educator they would like to be. This constant maneuvering is where teachers learn more about what makes them uniquely authentic. As they develop their practice with continuous self-assessment, the manifested identity will be authentic.

Figure 2.5 (page 42) illustrates the nested nature of these three layers.

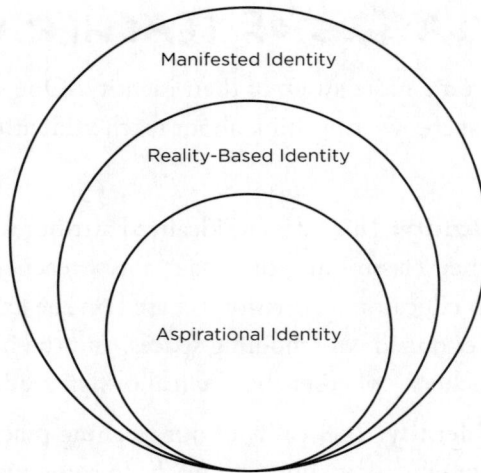

Figure 2.5: The three layers of teacher identity.

Figure 2.5 represents the intersection of the three layers associated with a teacher's identity. At the core is the identity we seek to manifest. We hold on to this sentiment as we navigate through reality with the goal of actualization. See the "Reflecting on Identity Layers" reproducible at the end of this chapter (page 50) to become acquainted with what the three layers of identity mean for you in pursuing authenticity in your teaching practice. In addition to using the reflection questions provided at the end of the chapter, we recommend that teachers try the following two strategies for unpacking their identity.

- **Role playing:** Role playing allows teachers to explore possible ideas or strategies related to their identity and practice before implementing them in the classroom. This process is sometimes called a "teach-back." The goal is to have the teacher simulate potential reactions and chart an appropriate course of action. Use the following ideas to get started.

  - Two teachers work together. One partner plays the role of a mentor, explaining their core teaching values to a new teacher. The mentee (another teacher) asks questions to delve deeper into these values. Once they've finished, they switch roles.

  - Imagine that a conflict arises between two students with different cultural backgrounds. Teachers role-play as mediators, guiding the students toward understanding and resolution. In the process, they learn about their own beliefs and cultural values.

- Teachers simulate situations that require them to address their own biases, such as preferring certain students over others. They role-play acknowledging and addressing these biases with a colleague or supervisor. This activity allows them to also consider why such a preference might exist.

- **Teacher vision board:** This activity involves reflective thinking, creative expression, and goal setting, allowing teachers to visualize and plan for the qualities and practices they aspire to embody in their professional roles. Teachers create a vision board (digital or print) that reflects their goals and aspirational identity. Once their vision board is complete, they create measurable goals to manifest the items they have created on their vision board. Use the following guided questions to get started.

  - Think about a teacher who inspired you. What qualities did they possess?

  - What values and principles do you want to uphold in your teaching practice?

  - How do you want your students to perceive you?

  - What teaching strategies and methods do you want to use in your classroom?

  - How do you want to handle challenges and conflicts?

Take a moment to reflect on what you've read in this section and consider the following questions: What next steps are emerging for you? How frequently do you navigate across all three layers of identity? How has each layer of your identity changed over time? What are the implications for your practice?

Think back to Ms. Xenos from chapter 1 (page 9). Through her coaching relationship with Jacobē, Ms. Xenos reflected on her aspirational and reality-based identities. Ms. Xenos aspired to be the teacher who is well loved by students yet holds them to high academic and behavioral expectations. She also aspired to be the teacher whose classroom students would love coming to because the content was relevant and engaging. Her current reality was that students loved her as a teacher, yet they often didn't accomplish as much work in her class as she'd like due to off-task behaviors. To facilitate the reflection process, Jacobē asked Ms. Xenos a series of clarifying questions.

Jacobē: Why do you think students aren't completing much work or paying attention?

> *A: (1) Because they don't find the content interesting, and (2) I don't always establish clear behavior expectations.*

Jacobē: Since we have a professional development series on your first point, let's zero in on your second point. I'm curious—why do you not always set clear expectations with students?

> *A: Because I don't want to be mean.*

Jacobē: Why do you think clear expectations equates to being mean?

> *A: Because some of the teachers that students seem to listen to the most are tough on kids and sometimes mean. It seems like the stricter you are, the more students behave.*

Jacobē: Why do you think kids listen to stricter teachers?

> *A: Because it is clear what the teacher wants from kids.*

Jacobē: What keeps you from making clear expectations like the teachers you reference?

> *A: I want kids to like me.*

Jacobē: So what I'm hearing you say is you'd like to create boundaries for students to meet expectations in ways that don't feel mean. Does this feel right? Let's dig in!

Through asking this series of why questions, Jacobē and Ms. Xenos were able to examine some assumptions and beliefs that Ms. Xenos held in relation to her aspirational and reality-based identities. This laid the foundation for Jacobē and Ms. Xenos to brainstorm action items that would help Ms. Xenos get to her manifested identity.

Let's connect the dots. Earlier in this chapter, we discussed the relationship between culture, cultural competence, and authentic teacher identities. In the example of Ms. Xenos, how might culture and cultural competence play a role in her ability to manifest great relationships with students *and* have a well-run classroom?

Understanding ourselves as complex beings is important to becoming an authentic educator who transcends the status quo. As a part of this iterative process, we need to consider the role our intersectional identities play in our authentic, manifested teacher identity.

UNPACKING THE INTERSECTIONALITY MATRIX

Now that we've looked at the aspirational, reality-based, and manifested levels of our teacher identity, let's circle back to intersectionality. Understanding intersectionality is an iterative process. We must constantly reflect on the larger categories that seek to classify who we are and consider the implications for our authentic teacher identity. We encourage you to think of intersectionality as a matrix. Various iterations of the matrix exist, many referred to as the matrix of domination (Collins, 2000, 2006). Figure 2.6 is our manifestation of it.

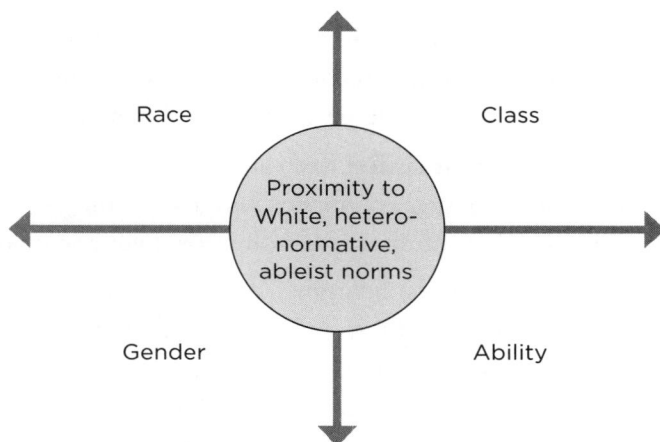

Figure 2.6: Intersectionality matrix.

The arrows between all four quadrants represent a person's capacity to move in any of the directions as it relates to the identity moniker we primarily consider when describing our attributes. Seeing intersectionality this way has profound implications for teachers. Recognizing that individuals embody multiple intersecting identities, as indicated by the arrows in figure 2.6, means acknowledging the complexity of their experiences and the various forms of privilege and oppression they may face. The further we move away from White, heteronormative, ableist norms, the more nuanced one's identity can become. Teachers can use this framework to better understand the complexity of their diverse backgrounds and tailor their pedagogical approach to foster inclusivity and equity in the classroom. The matrix challenges the tendency to categorize people based on only one aspect of their identity.

In unpacking their place in the matrix, teachers must take time to acknowledge the privilege they possess in each of these domains. In recognizing our privilege, we also conscientiously note the ways in which we might unintentionally oppress others.

How do teachers undertake this inner work? Consider the following ideas.

- **Engage in regular self-reflection:** Set aside dedicated time for introspection on the intersections of your own identity and consider how your various social categories (such as race, gender, class, and others) intersect and influence your experiences.

- **Seek diverse perspectives:** Actively seek out literature, media, and voices that represent diverse experiences and identities, and attend workshops, webinars, or events that focus on intersectionality to broaden your understanding.

- **Foster inclusive conversations:** Encourage open discussions with colleagues and peers about intersectionality, and create a safe space for sharing personal experiences and perspectives within a diverse group.

- **Stay informed on current issues:** Keep abreast of current events and societal issues related to intersectionality, and understand the broader context and implications of these issues on individuals and communities.

- **Evaluate teaching materials:** Scrutinize curriculum and teaching materials for inclusivity and representation; consider how different perspectives and experiences are portrayed in educational resources; foster a classroom environment where diverse perspectives are valued and explored; and reflect on your own comfort of teaching these materials and whether they allow for authentic presentation.

- **Embrace feedback and growth:** Welcome feedback on your understanding and application of intersectionality, and continuously seek opportunities for personal and professional growth in this area.

Figure 2.7 contains questions to consider as you continuously reflect on your intersections. These reflection questions provide teachers the opportunity to explore how intersectionality manifests in various aspects of their lives.

Reflecting on intersectionality prompts greater self-awareness and evolution. With evolution can come enhanced self-empathy and love. As we love ourselves as educators, we learn to see our students in a similar light—recognizing their identities in a more nuanced manner. We create an environment where authenticity can flourish.

Identity Moniker	Questions for Reflection
Race	• In what ways has your socially assigned race influenced your perception of the world? • In what ways has your socially assigned race afforded you particular privileges? In what ways has it oppressed you? How has this affected or impacted your sense of self? • How has your understanding of your socially assigned race changed over time? • Are there any cultural ideas or values you might associate with your identified race? • How are these cultural ideas or beliefs manifested in your teaching practice? Teacher identity? • How do your students respond to your race? If there are tensions, how do you reconcile these concerns? • What lived experiences were crucial to how you see your racial identity?
Gender	• In what ways has the gender assigned to you at birth influenced your perception of your abilities and your students' abilities? • In what ways has the gender assigned to you at birth shaped the experiences and opportunities you've had throughout your life? • What gender identity do you identify with? In what ways might this identity influence your instructional practice? • In what ways does your gender identity influence the relationships you have with students? • Have you ever been oppressed or privileged due to your gender identity? • Have you ever been oppressed or privileged due to your sexual identity? • How might you authentically and appropriately express your gender identity? • What culture(s) might you align to your chosen sexual or gender identity? What space exists for these elements in the classroom? Can students authentically connect with you through these mediums?

Figure 2.7: Reflection questions based on intersectionality identity markers.

continued →

Identity Moniker	Questions for Reflection
Class	• How do you define the idea of social and economic class?
	• What social and economic classes do you identify with?
	• What social and economic classes were you born into? Which ones did you spend most of your formative years a part of? Which do you now identify with?
	• What culture(s) and or cultural ideas do you associate with the social and economic class(es) you identify with?
	• Based on your social and economic class, what do you believe is the purpose of school? How does this align to your teacher identity?
	• Based on your social and economic class, how do you perceive the students you support? What narratives have been shared about those who have a different class than you?
	• Given your lived experiences, what "counts" as knowledge? What doesn't?
	• What ideas did you encounter about class during your upbringing?
	• What relationships do you see between class and race? Explain your thinking.
Ability	• How do ability, physical needs, or neurodiversity affect your identity?
	• What learning and lived experiences have influenced your understanding of your ability? How do you feel society views your ability?
	• In what ways have your abilities privileged you? In what ways have you experienced oppression due to your abilities?
	• What connections do you make between your ability, race, gender, and class? How would you describe the intersection of these identities?
	• How do you want your students to perceive your ability? How might you leverage your ability as a means for building authentic relationships with students?

SUMMING UP

When teachers step back and examine the layers of their identity, they begin to manifest an authentic identity in the classroom. By understanding who they are and how their identities influence their relationship to others—particularly their students—they gain a more nuanced understanding of culture and identity in the classroom community. This evolving cultural competence allows them show up with authenticity. And from that posture of authenticity, they are empowered to disrupt inequities in the classroom.

Consider the following key takeaways from this chapter.

- Our identities are deeply interconnected and cannot be separated into larger categories. This connection is known as intersectionality.

- Intersectionality is also connected to the concept of culture. Culture is known as big-*C* or surface, shallow Culture and little-*c* or deeper, subterranean culture.

- Cultural competence is the ability to successfully teach students who come from a different culture than our own. It entails developing certain personal and interpersonal awareness of our identities that allows us to become more critically conscious, which is the foundation for disrupting inequities.

- Our brains often want us to classify and categorize people based on our own lived experiences, but these lived experiences are not always universal.

- When we begin to unpack the nuance and layers of who we are, we can then manifest a true or authentic identity within classroom spaces. By manifesting our authentic identity in our classrooms, we then can begin to approach our teaching and our students with an increased awareness of cultural competence, which in turn will allow us to begin disrupting inequities in our classrooms.

Reflecting on Identity Layers

Read the following journal prompts about the three layers of identity you read about in chapter 2 and record your responses in the space provided.

Aspirational Identity

A teacher's aspirational identity is their ideal vision for who they want to be as an educator.

Name teachers who had an impact on your learning.

Which teachers do you wish to emulate? Why?

What is your vision for the climate and culture of your classroom? How does this connect to your authentic self?

How do you expect or hope students will respond to you?

What elements of yourself do you wish to share with students?

What elements of yourself and your identity are completely off-limits?

What intersections or cultures do you belong to? How might these elements of yourself show up in the classroom (whether intentionally or unintentionally)?

Reality-Based Identity

A teacher's *reality-based identity* is the version of themselves embodied in their teaching practice, which is contingent on the context in which they choose to teach.

How do your students see you as a teacher? Is it the same as how you see yourself? Why or why not?

What do you need to learn about your students?

What lived experiences have prepared you for your current teaching context?

What do you still need to learn?

What assumptions do you hold about your current context? About students? Where do these assumptions stem from?

What are the cultures and intersections of your students? How do these cultures and intersections compare to your own experiences?

What do you need to learn more about with respect to culture and intersectionality of your school context?

Manifested Identity

A teacher's *manifested identity* is the intentional implementation and execution of their authentic teacher identity, which is likely a hybrid of the aspirational and reality-based identities.

What changes will you make to present a more authentic self to your students?

How might students support your development as an educator? As a person?

How does your manifested identity compare and contrast to the aspirational identity you hold?

How would you reconcile your aspirational identity with your manifested identity?

Which of the two identities is preferable to your students? Which of the two do they believe is more authentically aligned to you?

CHAPTER 3

THE SYSTEM AND AUTHENTICITY

When Reshma started her career in education, she was a volunteer with Junior Achievement—an organization that designs learning activities to help students understand their communities, tap into financial literacy, and unpack the idea of civic engagement. In tandem with this, she was a substitute teacher in Florida. During her time in the classroom, she took a common approach to instruction. She came in, introduced herself, taught the lesson through direct instruction, did some checks for understanding, and called it a day. At eighteen, why would she think of doing anything differently? This is the way her teachers taught her, and it's likely how their teachers taught them. She taught by default rather than by conscious choice.

Anthony S. Bryk (2010), president of the Carnegie Foundation for the Advancement of Teaching and pioneer of improvement science practices in schools, often says that systems are *designed* to produce the outcomes that they do. In Reshma's case, her K–12 experiences (the system) created the teaching practices she initially adhered to as a novice teacher (the outcomes). Systems in education are representative of larger histories and narratives; they aren't isolated entities at any one moment in time.

In the previous chapter, we discussed the notion of identity, culture, and inter-sectionality. Schooling as a system plays a profound role in the development of these attributes. In this chapter we explore the concept of systems, the purpose they serve, connections to racist ideologies in schooling, and the implications for teachers' authenticity.

Guiding Questions

- What are explicit and implicit systems that exist within education or learning spaces?
- How has the structure of schooling reinforced behaviors relating to the practice of learning?
- How is zero-sum thinking related to systems within schools?
- How have we been conditioned or socialized to perceive schooling systems?
- What roles does equity play in our aspirations to address racialized systems?

DEFINING THE SYSTEM

What do we mean when we talk about *the system* in the context of education? Educator Frank Betts (1992) posits that "a system is a set of elements that function as a whole to achieve a common purpose. A *subsystem* is a component of a larger system; for example, the circulatory system is a subsystem of a human system." Researchers Anthony S. Bryk, Louis M. Gomez, Alicia Grunow, and Paul G. LeMahieu (2015) affirm this concept when he discusses the intricacies of school systems and how many learning experiences are not designed with the user, namely students and teachers, in mind. Schools as a system are open, meaning that schools engage in a symbiotic relationship with legal and social mandates that have an idealized or aspirational outcome. Take, for example, *Brown v. Board of Education of Topeka* (1954). This court case sought to disrupt the segregated approach to education that had long existed in the United States. Table 3.1 breaks down how this case aspired to create equitable education outcomes.

Notice the interplay of systems within this example. The federal government operates as a system to uphold particular laws and practices. This system then connects to the subsystem of schools, which have their own practices and expectations. Once the federal system shifted its policies, schools were forced to adjust their practice. These shifts impacted the social system within schools, prompting additional systemic shifts. Building on the information provided in the table, additional systemic shifts within schools included the creation of a predominantly White and female teaching force, the tracking of students, and the funneling of students into special education programs if their behaviors did not meet a particular teacher's criteria for acceptable behavior (Alexander, 2012). Schools are technically integrated, but many of the subsystems remain stagnant, given their origins.

Table 3.1: Example of Synthesis Between Sociopolitical Systems and Schools

Legal mandate	The Supreme Court ruled that racially segregated schools were inherently unconstitutional and violated the Fourteenth Amendment. This case essentially upended the 1896 case of *Plessy v. Ferguson* in which institutions could create racially segregated "separate but equal" spaces.
Social mandate	The social mandate is inextricably linked to the legal mandate. Consider the following immediate expectations that are inextricably linked to equitable outcomes. • Students should have the opportunity to learn with peers who might be racially different. • Schools and similar institutions should have access to the same resources (financial, emotional, social, and so on). • The quality of education should be equitable at all institutions regardless of the racial demographic in attendance.
Aspirational outcomes	There were several aspirational outcomes for the integration of schools, such as the following. • Equitable access to resources and materials, especially for Black students. • Humanization of Black students in order to have their lives and voices valued. • Dismantling of explicitly segregated spaces to ensure equitable access for all.
Actual impact on systems	While the aspirational outcomes did manifest in tangible laws and physical experiences, subtle and subversive shifts modified the system in ways that perpetuated inequitable outcomes. • De facto segregation: the movement of White people away from communities of color, thereby taking resources with them, sometimes called White flight. • Stereotyping or dehumanizing Black students and those of the global majority as having particular assumptions around school. • Underfunding and standardizing schools to remove opportunities for additional learning and exploration of skills. • Teaching and learning became inextricably linked to White supremacist values with little to no regard for other cultural modes of thinking (Givens, 2021).

Schools in the United States have served numerous purposes throughout the evo-lution of the public education system. At the onset, schools served the aim of cre-ating a continued economic stratification of learned gentlemen who would go on to maintain the status quo. When schooling became accessible to all people, it was reflective of the economic and social needs of the time. Educational historians have varying perspectives on this, but most agree that the accessibility of schooling in the early 20th century was aligned with the influx of immigrants and an aspiration to codify what is meant to be American and participate in American policies, practices, and culture (for example, democracy; Neem, 2017). It wasn't until World War II that the high school diploma carried the weight it does today. Now, education systems largely adhere to these antiquated systems that further produce inequitable outcomes (such as bell schedules, direct instruction, row-based setting, standardized tests, and so on; Petty & Leach, 2020; powell, n.d.; Safir & Dugan, 2021). The systems that currently exist within schools as well as the systems that control schooling practices have not updated to reflect the contemporary needs of students. This means that as adults, we spent our most formative years in systems that perpetuated ideologies that potentially stripped away our authenticity.

Inequity in public education is perhaps most pronounced with regard to race. Legal protections against racism have only existed in the United States for the last fifty-eight years, as of the writing of this book. Many of the people who witnessed this transition are still living. There is an entire generation of adults who lived through systematic shifts that sought to create an anti-racist society. These systemic shifts color how people view the importance of race to schooling systems; they seep into our individual and collective conscious and unconscious beliefs through socialization.

Table 3.2, adapted from john a. powell (n.d.), visualizes the connection between larger sociopolitical systems related to race and the impact on schools.

The chief executive officer of Cengage, Michael Hansen (2021), stated in a recent *Harvard Business Review* article, "This archaic [education] system simply no longer works in our modern world. The U.S. education system must be reevaluated to better prepare students with employable skills." Hansen, while well intentioned in his indignation around student preparedness, is still writing within a paradigm that sees schools as a launching pad with the end goal of creating workers. Paulo Freire (1968/2000) described such practices as the oppressed becoming the oppressors: minimizing the opportunity for creating, dreaming, and liberation. As you can see, there is a cyclical, repetitive process to the ways in which sociopolitical systems per-petuate systemic practices within school and vice versa.

Table 3.2: Sociopolitical Factors' Impact on School Systems

Sociopolitical Factors	Impact on School Systems
• De facto segregation • *A Nation at Risk* (1983) panic in reference to declining literacy and mathematics proficiency scores • Concentrated poverty	• Reduced per-pupil spending and resources. Larger class sizes, reduced materials, teacher capacity, and so on. • Overtesting and legislation supporting measurement in the form of assessments (Every Student Succeeds Act, 2015; No Child Left Behind, 2001). • Nonexistent structures to support students' basic physical and emotional needs (for example, food, laundromats, and so on). Think Abraham Maslow's (1943) hierarchy.

The current system creates inequitable outcomes through funding disparities, standardized testing, unequal access to great teachers, resource disparities, bias, and Eurocentric curriculum just to name a few. These problems with the current system hinder a teacher's ability to walk in authenticity. If teachers are not careful, the system can allow us to unwittingly harm ourselves or others. That's why, as teachers, it's important to reflect on the things that impact us and our schools. These systemic challenges not only impede a teacher's capacity to authentically engage with students but also pose the risk of unintentional harm to individuals within the educational community. Vigilance in reflecting on these impactful factors is paramount. By fostering awareness and advocating for change, educators can strive toward a more equitable and inclusive system that allows teachers to authentically connect with their students and collectively work toward a more just educational landscape.

RECOGNIZING SYSTEMS AND THE USER

Our book centers on two users: teachers and students. These individuals are crucial to the ways in which we envision and enact schools. Teachers are responsible for delivering high-quality instruction to students. They possess subject-specific knowledge and pedagogical skills to design engaging lessons, facilitate learning experiences, and adapt their teaching methods to meet the diverse needs of students. Their knowledge, skills, dedication, and nurturing approach contribute to creating a positive, engaging, and effective learning environment. Recognizing the significance of teachers in the education system is essential for building successful schools and fostering the academic and personal growth of students.

Equally, students are the recipients of teachers' expertise and interactions. Students are meant to be the beneficiaries of educational systems, although those systems are conditioned by larger social and political aspirations. It is essential to recognize and critically examine how educational systems impact both students and teachers. Understanding these dynamics can help identify areas for improvement and work toward creating inclusive, equitable, and student-centered educational environments. By leaning into authenticity and acknowledging the reciprocal relationship between students, teachers, and the larger educational systems, it becomes possible to strive for meaningful and positive changes that enhance the educational experience for all.

TRANSFORMING EDUCATION TOWARD EQUITY

The method for escaping and disrupting problematic systems is through the lens of equity. We define *equity* as the creation of practices, policies, and expectations that support the advancement of all people based on their needs and readiness (Tomlinson, 2014). Equity acknowledges lived experiences and backgrounds that can both privilege and hinder advancement.

Whereas systems valuing competition pit people against each other, systems valuing equity humanize people and seek to find methods for rectifying injustices and seeking liberation. Table 3.3 provides an example of how a common system within schools, the attendance system, that may perpetuate oppression can be reformed to support liberation.

Table 3.3: Reforming a School System to Support Liberation

System Paradigm	Description
Element	Attendance is a common system and structure within schools. The practice, used to identify which students are in attendance as well as those who are late to class, can also be used as a tool to target students in a punitive manner.
Common Pitfall	Some students experience obstacles that impact their attendance and lead to tardiness, including: • Inconsistent access to transportation to and from school • Responsibility to care for younger siblings • No access to clean clothes or laundry facilities • Conflicting schedules with parents

System Paradigm	Description
Status Quo Intervention	In response to poor attendance or frequent tardiness, teachers operating in the status quo system may: • Retain students based on their attendance • Provide completion or failure grades based on presence in class • Adopt a narrative that students or their families are not interested in school
Equity-Focused Intervention	Teachers and administrators desiring to transform the status quo system toward an equity-based system may: • Partner with local laundering services to provide wash cards or similar services • Partner with local transportation services to provide timely access to school • Create childcare facilities or services within a school so students might be able to bring younger siblings to school with them • Develop a modified schedule or start times to help students get to school on time or leave early to support childcare

Equity, when placed at the center of school design and systems, centers on the user (Bryk, 2020). Who is the user? The user is primarily students, but also teachers, leaders, and other faculty who are responsible for young people's education. Unfortunately, systems do not always consider the user but rather sometimes consider the intended outcome or desire. If systems do consider the user, sometimes it's in ways that just use the user, such as continually gathering information from the user but not involving them in the decision-making process (High Tech High Unboxed, 2024). Bryk (2010) argues that for schools to truly rethink educational systems, several variables need to be in place. Table 3.4 (page 62) explores these variables and the impact they can have on rethinking potentially oppressive systems.

Table 3.4: Variables for Addressing Oppressive School Systems

Variable	Description	How This Impacts Systems
Coherent Instructional Guidance System	In some contexts, this is known as the instructional foundation. Schools should have a clear operational framework, typically in the form of curricula, that drives the instructional and assessment experience for students. This content can be modified to support the needs of neurodiverse learners. Teachers retain autonomy in how they teach the curricular materials.	Having a strong curricular road map for what to teach and how to teach relevant content ensures: • Content can be modified to be culturally responsive to students' needs • Intellectual prep can encompass the modification of information to meet the needs of neurodiverse learners • Teachers are teaching with intentionality and agency
Professional Capacity	Educators should strive to be continuously recursive and willing to learn. While not all professional development is useful, the mental space and scheduling aspects must be in place to support continued learning.	Professional capacity allows teachers to: • Question or challenge existing systems with the support of research and inquiry • Be seen as experts as opposed to receptacles of "top down" information • Ideate and generate innovative ideas that disrupt the status quo
Strong Parent-Community-School Ties	Relationships between schools and communities are often transactional within the status quo system. Authentic parent or community relationships have been shown to have a positive impact on teachers' practice and students' overall achievement.	Taking a proactive (as opposed to transactional) approach to relationships with school partners allows for true collaboration. This can disrupt systems by: • Integrating the assets of a community into all aspects of schooling • Supporting students who are struggling and not meeting other systemic expectations (grades, attendance, and so on) • Offering experiences that leverage the talents of community members

Variable	Description	How This Impacts Systems
Student-Centered Learning Climate	Students are the ultimate recipients of school-system outcomes. Status quo systems are not designed with the student in mind. Cultivating a climate that invites student voice ensures that system reform focuses on meeting students' holistic needs.	Creating structures that regularly invite student voice ensures: • Students can challenge a system or structure they find to be inequitable • Systems and practices become authentic to students' needs and dreams. • Teacher investment or buy-in around necessary systems or practices (for example, curricular changes).
Leadership Drives Change	Strong leaders or leadership teams are crucial to any school. Leaders set the pulse for the school and its expectations of students. They also help to design and reinforce many of the existing systems.	As leaders are ultimately responsible for the systems and structures within schools, their involvement can: • Ensure alignment and coherence across all systems • Establish a clear bar and foundation for educational excellence • Determine structures for accountability if aspiring to establish an anti-racist approach to teaching and learning

Think back to the introduction to this chapter where you read about Reshma's experience as a novice teacher. The system conditioned her to focus on whether her own practice aligned with the expectations of the status quo system rather than on meeting the unique needs of her students. She was expected to teach a particular lesson with little regard for the intended recipients. Even well-intentioned systems can be problematic if they do not consider those who are the most impacted. It's key for teachers pursuing authenticity to understand these systems, their origins, and the impacts they aim to have on reforming the system toward greater equity.

Pause and Ponder

Pause and ponder the following questions considering what you've read.

- What systems have the most impact on your identity?
- How would you define the concept of equity? How does it manifest in your aspirational identity?
- What systems within your locus of control might you adjust to have an equity-oriented lens?

BEING THE TEACHER YOU STRIVE TO BE

The average teacher doesn't wake up one morning and arbitrarily decide to go into education. In fact, most educators aspire to become teachers because they are influenced by an exemplary teacher or motivated by a teacher who unintentionally inflicted harm (Ramkellawan-Arteaga, 2017). Teachers of all experiences and backgrounds typically enter the field replicating practices and beliefs they have been conditioned and socialized to value. These experiences shape their perspectives on teaching and learning and can influence the ways in which they replicate or challenge existing educational systems and practices.

Socialization plays a crucial role in this process. Teachers are socialized into the profession through their formal education, teacher preparation programs, and the school cultures in which they work. They absorb explicit and implicit messages about teaching, curriculum, assessment, and classroom management, which are often deeply embedded in the educational systems they operate within (Harro, 2000). There are often two systems at play when thinking about the ways in which teachers are socialized: overt and subtle structures.

Overt systems refer to the visible and explicit structures, policies, and practices within a school or educational system. These may include curriculum frameworks, grading policies, discipline procedures, standardized testing requirements, and professional development programs. Teachers may consciously engage with these systems and adapt their practices to align with them. *Subtle* systems, on the other hand, are less apparent and may involve underlying assumptions, power dynamics, and cultural norms that shape the educational environment. These can include beliefs about student abilities, gender roles, racial biases, or implicit expectations for behavior and academic performance. Subtle systems can perpetuate inequities or reinforce certain social, cultural, or ideological values.

Reflecting on the systems at play within a school can be a valuable exercise for teachers and educational leaders as it encourages a recursive unpacking of how we have become the educators that we are. Teachers must probe the systems that have both benefitted and hindered their authenticity and can proactively consider the ways in which they might adjust course. It allows them to become aware of the influences shaping their beliefs and practices and critically examine the impact of these systems on student outcomes and experiences. By actively questioning and engaging with the systems, teachers work toward creating more inclusive, equitable, and student-centered educational environments.

Figure 3.1 (page 66) models how one educator reflects on existing systems, the impact on their beliefs, and how they dream about a new future. To complete this activity for yourself, use the reproducible "Unpacking Internalized Beliefs" at the end of this chapter (page 81).

The purpose of this tool is to consider opportunities for rethinking school systems that are harmful to young people and educators. We often hear teachers give voice to larger initiatives or ideas they cannot control. We have also heard educators express a desire to rethink practices that have been long held either by themselves or by others. With the aid of this resource, teachers can consider the ways in which they would address an inequitable system while simultaneously reflecting on internalized beliefs related to education.

As teachers engage in this reflection process, they must also consider the following guiding questions.

- What am I willing to relinquish or renegotiate to create a system that is more equitable for my students?

- How does my reflection or ideas lean into or push up against anti-racist ideology?

Instructions: This exercise invites you to examine the systems at work within your educational context, recognize beliefs you've internalized as a result of the culture of these systems, and then consciously dream a new way of being that reforms the system. Consider the following questions associated with each prompt and write a response in the space provided.

System Name

- What system or subsystem do I recognize at play in my educational context?

Internalized Beliefs

- What beliefs or stories do I hold that are informed by this system?
- How does it appear in my current practice?
- Where do these beliefs come from?
- In response to these beliefs, am I consciously disrupting oppressive practices or unintentionally perpetuating them?

Dream and Reimagine

- If I could reimagine this system, what would it entail?
- How does my reimagined version compare to my current practice?
- What action can I take to enact this dream?

System Name	Internalized Beliefs	Dream and Reimagine
The use of standardized assessments in school as a measure of achievement	There is some value to the use of standardized assessments in schools. It helps teachers to understand and appreciate what they should teach as well as how they teach it. This belief comes from seeing teachers teach content that was not assessed or taking a class that was completely disconnected from the subsequent Regents exam—a high-stakes assessment administered to New York State high school students in multiple content areas. Unfortunately, it does not take into account learner variability, and standardized assessments are often used by districts as the "end all" measure of a student's worth.	In an ideal environment, we would return to the use of student portfolios as a means for measuring student achievement. This, in tandem to standardized measures, would allow evaluators to determine student readiness for advancement. It would also allow for a more holistic view of what a student is capable of. This would require norming on the quality and expectations of portfolios, determining the attributes and essential pieces of each portfolio, and revising curricular practice to reflect the needs of the portfolio.

Figure 3.1: Unpacking internalized systems sample worksheet.

*Visit **go.SolutionTree.com/diversityandequity** for a free reproducible version of this figure.*

LEARNING FROM YOUR STUDENTS

When was the last time you had a deep, personal, intentional conversation with a student? When was the last time you asked a student for feedback or advice on a lesson or forthcoming topic and genuinely wanted to hear their answer? In his foreword for the book *Street Data*, Christopher Emdin (2021a) writes about a question he frequently receives: Why do young people from urban settings have such a hard time in traditional classrooms? He explains:

> There are considerations beyond the rigors of the subject matter that lead to what many term as underperformance. It may not be that the academic content is too rigorous. It may mean that the manner of delivery is too simplistic and therefore, disengaging. (Emdin 2021a, p. xiii)

There are two systems that Emdin (2021a) refers to in this quote. The first system is the use of traditional, teacher-centered approaches to instruction. The second system is the mode of assessment, which carries implications around a student's perceived academic worth or readiness. The fusion of these systems creates a narrative or story that is perpetuated at various levels of a system and internalized by those who are within it. Underperformance by Black- and Brown-bodied students often results in a narrative that these students internalize. This narrative results in an identity that has been forced on the students well before they can begin to articulate their own sense of self (D. Gray, Hope, & Byrd, 2020). A forced identity coupled with school systems that are meant to strip autonomy, inquiry, and agency perpetuates cycles of inequity.

School zero-tolerance policies (for example, behavior management systems) that police young people and reinforce the school-to-prison pipeline (Alexander, 2012) are a good example of a system of forced identity perpetuating inequity. Conversely:

> When Black youth have cultural socialization experiences in schools (e.g., being taught about the historical contributions of Black people in a particular field or discipline), they learn about the many ways and milieus in which Blackness is consistent with academic excellence, and they can imagine themselves as active contributors to the school environment. (D. Gray et al., 2020)

The systems within a school must be designed with intentionality toward fostering cultural experiences that affirm Black youth and other students holding historically marginalized identities. This means rethinking the role of joy and identity within schools, especially within instructional systems.

Rather than placing a narrative on students, teachers must develop habits and routines that invite students to create their own narratives, to co-create their experience in the classroom. Educators should cultivate habits and routines that encourage students to shape their own stories, to collaboratively construct their classroom experience and thereby shift existing narratives. Figure 3.2 (page 68) offers a series of questions teachers can use to learn more about how students perceive themselves as learners and, more importantly, as human beings. Teachers can use these questions for self-reflection as well as student feedback. Note that this figure is designed with space to transcribe notes from conversations with students.

Guiding Questions	Student Responses
Teaching and Learning Systems • Do you feel represented or seen in your classes and lessons? • How can your teachers respond to your needs as a learner? • What are some of your favorite activities to do in class? • How interested are you in class? What is interesting about this class? What might make it more interesting? • Do you believe that your teachers are fair in their grading policies?	
Behavior Management Systems • How do you feel about your school's policies around behavior? Do you feel that they are equitable? • How do your teachers use some of the behavior management techniques or systems in their class? • Do your teachers celebrate your strengths or good behaviors? • Do your teachers attempt to build relationships with you and your peers?	
Impact on Self and Identity • Have you ever felt like you were less than or inferior to your peers? Why or why not? • How do you see yourself in school? • Do you have positive experiences with school? Why or why not? • Do you believe in yourself? Why or why not? What role do you think school has played in this?	

Figure 3.2: Unpacking student perspectives of systems.

Visit go.SolutionTree.com/diversityandequity for a free reproducible version of this figure.

The three domains in figure 3.2 are typically the areas where our internalized beliefs become explicit. As we learn to become more authentic, it is crucial to gain insight from students with respect to how they see these systems. Greater awareness allows us to move with intentionality.

There are students who are adept at "doing school." They know how to behave and present in a manner that might be pleasing to educators. These students can get all the A's on the exams and are socially adept. Students who excel at "doing school" often navigate the educational system successfully by meeting academic and behavioral expectations. They may receive praise and recognition for their performance, but their authentic selves may be overlooked or suppressed in the process. Conversely, students who do not engage in performative behaviors related to school can be more authentic. They might also be subject to harsher consequences from inequitable systems. Take, for example, the B-average student who is obsessed with sneakers. She loves skirting the school's uniform policy to show off the latest pair of kicks, arriving at school in uniform except for her shoes. As a result, the behavior system mandates that she receive detention. She doesn't mind because of the joy of wearing the shoes she was so excited to get when they were released. Teachers, not having a relationship with this student or understanding this context, might mischaracterize her as a bad student, but there is nothing objectively wrong with being a B-average student.

The joy derived from wearing recently released shoes indicates a personal and positive context that might not be immediately apparent to teachers and all those within the school system. The system requires "equality" and therefore would seek to collectively punish the student instead of celebrating her authenticity.

The problem lies in the system's inability to recognize and respond to the complexities of individual experiences and expressions of joy within the school environment. In this example alone, we can see how the system can strip away one's authenticity and identity. Think about a time where you were misunderstood in school like this student. How did it impact who you are today?

It is crucial for schools to critically examine their systems and subsequent policies to ensure they are fair and equitable. Fair and equitable for all students means we are thinking about the needs of students who might not be on our immediate radar or periphery—that is, the students who are quiet or might have average assessment scores. Those are the students whose voices we need to hear.

By taking into account the individual circumstances, cultural perspectives, and personal interests of students, schools can develop policies that promote inclusivity while still maintaining order and safety. By promoting a student-centered approach that appreciates and celebrates the unique identities and interests of students, educators can create an environment where all students feel valued and supported, irrespective of their conformity to performative behaviors or their deviation from the expected norms.

It is important to note the way in which a system can influence one's approach to students. Systems, especially those grounded in racist ideologies, often espouse a zero-sum approach to its structures. In the following sections, we make the connection between zero-sum thinking and true change within schools.

SEEING ZERO-SUM THINKING AS A BARRIER TO CHANGE

One major thing that impacts an educator's ability to present in authentic ways is zero-sum thinking. *Zero-sum thinking*—when a person perceives a situation as one person's gain would be another's loss—hurts transformation of societal systems. For example, when considering police accountability, many folks have binary thinking of either we need to reform it, or we need to keep it as is. During 2020, Blue Lives Matter flags became as ubiquitous as Black Lives Matter paraphernalia. The sentiment was that one could not support Black lives without being anti-police and vice versa. The polarization of politics along these lines was ferocious. *It did not have to be this way.* More than one thing can be true at a time. A person can think critically about law enforcement culture, policies, and practices and advocate for change and not be anti-police at the same time. Zero-sum thinking is a fallacy.

This zero-sum or binary thinking is deeply ingrained in American history and society. In her book *The Sum of Us: What Racism Costs Everyone and How We Can Prosper Together*, McGhee (2021) traces how no one wins when racism is at play. One example she names is that when desegregation occurred, many cities that had public pools closed them, filled the pools with dirt, or intimidated people of color from coming to the pools rather than integrate the pools (McGhee, 2021). Such decisions impacted everyone. McGhee states, "Uncomprehending white children cried as the city contractors poured dirt in the pool, paved it over, and seeded it with grass that was green by the time summer came around" (p. 25). Community leaders who saw Black members of the community gaining access to pools as a loss for the White community rather than a benefit to everyone in the community are a classic example of zero-sum thinking.

Pause and Ponder

Pause and ponder the following question considering what you've read.

- Where in society do you observe the story that "progress for people of color must come at the expense of White people" being communicated, and by whom?
- What are some examples of zero-sum thinking you see in school systems?
- How has zero-sum thinking impacted your understanding of yourself?

Not only does zero-sum thinking hurt society at large, but it also impacts the education system. Many educators and schools have a hard time cultivating schools that work for all learners because many times educational opportunities are thought of as a zero-sum construct. Through this thinking lens:

> Equity can't be conceptualized as fair because the perceived finite nature of opportunity makes it impossible to differentiate support without underserving some part of the population. This is exactly why equity is such a profound challenging concept because it is often presented to us in practice as a zero-sum game scenario. (Stembridge, 2020, pp. 8–9)

For example, some think that to operationalize more inclusive, culturally relevant teaching and outcomes in schools, the learning standards must be lowered. Some educators internalize this narrative and don't give students the opportunity to have their needs met. Thus, both the educator and the student feel unsuccessful. For example, one of the schools Jacobē previously worked for wanted to stop the unit they were currently teaching to focus on standardized test preparation. Jacobē advised them to integrate the skills students need for the state test into their normal units of study. The school leaders at this school felt like if they focused on integrating the skills it would be good for students who were already on grade level, but it would come at the expense of progress for the students who were approaching grade level. Thus zero-sum thinking surrounding standardized tests in this example manifested from the following.

- **Narrowing the focus of instruction:** It placed a disproportionate emphasis on test scores as the sole measure of educational success. It led to an overreliance on high-stakes testing and neglected other valuable aspects of education, such as critical thinking, creativity, and problem-solving skills.

- **Neglecting the multiple ways learners can demonstrate knowledge:** It privileged one way of assessment and devalued alternative assessment methods and limited educational approaches that cater to individual student needs.

- **Stigmatization of lower-performing groups:** It perpetuated the stigma of students at the margins and led to the perception that students on the margins are inherently less capable or deserving of quality education and resources.

The effect of this decision helped maintain the status quo, where those on the margins receive more narrow instruction while those more privileged receive instruction that prepares them to be leaders in society. An alternate and equity-centered approach might see the following structures in place: students create goals based on their readiness, teachers include curriculum that centers standards through relevant content, and classrooms include instructional stations (Muhammad, 2023). This is just one small example of how we can move away from zero-sum thinking. We must see the system and how it leans into zero-sum thinking as a barrier to school change. It limits possibilities, stifles innovation, and perpetuates the status quo. Zero-sum thinking can maintain the status quo in education more generally through the following.

- **Limited resource allocation:** Zero-sum thinking assumes that resources, such as funding, staff, or time, are fixed and finite. This mindset leads to competition among different stakeholders for limited resources, making it difficult to allocate resources effectively to support meaningful change initiatives.

- **Resistance to change:** Zero-sum thinking fosters a mindset of winners and losers, where any change is perceived as a threat to someone's interests or status. This can create resistance from individuals or groups who fear losing out or believe that change will diminish their own influence or control.

- **Lack of collaboration:** Zero-sum thinking encourages a mindset of competition rather than collaboration. Stakeholders may be reluctant to work together or share ideas and resources, fearing that doing so will weaken their own position or advantage.

- **Inertia and complacency:** Zero-sum thinking reinforces the notion that maintaining the status quo is the safest approach. It discourages risk taking and experimentation, as any change is viewed as a zero-sum game with potential losses. This can lead to stagnation and the perpetuation of outdated practices.

- **Failure to address systemic issues:** Zero-sum thinking tends to focus on individual gains or losses rather than addressing broader systemic issues. It may overlook the need for structural changes or transformative approaches that address inequities and improve overall educational outcomes.

- **Lack of innovation and creativity:** Zero-sum thinking stifles innovation and creative problem solving. When the belief is that resources are limited, there is little room for exploring new ideas or approaches that could potentially bring about positive change.

To overcome these barriers imposed by zero-sum thinking and promote school change, educators must transcend the zero-sum mindset and begin to take action rooted in the possibility of *both/and*. This involves embracing collaboration, seeking win-win solutions, and recognizing that change can lead to collective benefits. It requires reframing challenges as opportunities for growth and embracing a mindset that focuses on shared goals, innovation, and continuous improvement.

TRANSCENDING ZERO-SUM THINKING

Educators must transform the system to be *positive sum*, or a situation in which "resources are somehow increased and an approach is formulated in which the desires and needs of all concerned are satisfied" (The Editors of Encyclopaedia Britannica, 2024). To do this we must lean into endemic ways of being and seeing the world, such as cultural respect and recognition, collaboration and partnership, community-centric values, and a holistic perspective that considers the interconnectedness of all things. The endemic way often overlaps with positive-sum thinking in their shared emphasis on interconnectedness, collaboration, and the creation of value that benefits everyone involved. Both perspectives promote a mindset that moves beyond zero-sum competition and toward cooperative, inclusive approaches that contribute to the well-being of individuals, communities, and the broader world.

The National Indian Child Welfare Association writes:

> On our globe today, there are two prominent worldviews—linear and relational. The linear worldview is rooted in European and mainstream American thought. It is very temporal and is firmly rooted in the logic that says cause has to come before effect. In contrast, the relational worldview sees life as harmonious relationships where health is achieved by maintaining balance between the many interrelating factors in one's circle of life. (as cited in Safir & Dugan, 2021, pp. 16–17)

In education this can look like only some knowledge counting or like only one way to demonstrate a competency like standardized assessments, which are rooted in Eurocentric ways of knowing. Eurocentric or Western ways of knowing also value individualism, the scientific, and one truth and are skeptical of the spiritual. Indigenous ways of being, in contrast, embrace the values of oral knowledge, all life mattering, community, and holism—a stance that interweaves all aspects of learning such as the mind, heart, body, and spirit as interconnected, inseparable, and drawing from cultural wealth and ancestral knowledge (Safir & Dugan, 2021).

Figure 3.3 (page 74) represents some of the core stances that we as educators must embrace to operate in a positive-sum paradigm.

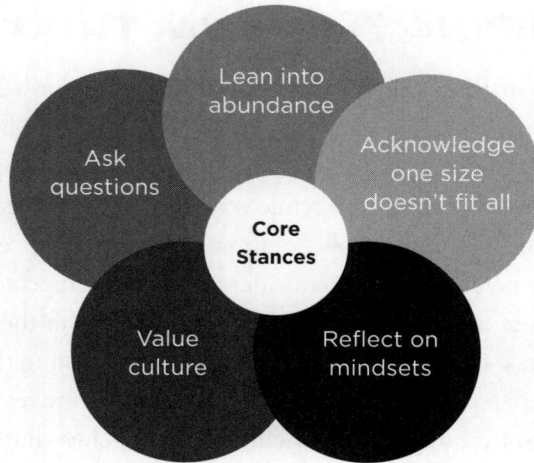

Figure 3.3: Positive-sum stances.

Let's look at each of these core stances in more detail.

- **Lean into abundance:** There is enough for everyone to prosper. Together we go far. McGhee (2021) argues that the "solidarity dividend," or gains made when people come together across race, benefits everyone. So let's come together as a collective and fight for the liberation of everyone. Abundance starts with a value and belief that there is more available to us. In schools, this looks like providing opportunities (for example, classes, extracurriculars) to all students, regardless of our assumptions. A high school in upstate New York allows students to self-select into Advanced Placement (AP) classes. The student (rather than the educator) can choose if it is a good fit. Let's see beyond what is right in front of our nose and expand our view.

- **Ask questions:** Learn about perspectives that are different from yours. Start by listening. To operate beyond zero-sum thinking we must ask yourselves and each other, particularly students, questions. When a binary presents itself, we must consider, is there a way both can be true? What perspectives are we missing? Who are we potentially harming in these binaries? How can we move beyond the binaries? Is there a situation in which we can benefit everyone in a non-savior way? We must look for more options or solutions. Interrogating the options and considering more than what's right in front of us is important.

- **Value culture:** When moving past zero-sum thinking, considering culture is paramount. If culture is not considered, then it is impossible for folks with different cultural knowledge to come together and not marginalize someone of a different culture. We must see the beauty and the humanity in each other. We must believe that every life has value. We must shift culture and language where it belongs, the community. Doing so will cultivate schools where all students can feel seen and affirmed.

- **Reflect on mindsets:** Mindsets and change are hard, yet to operate beyond zero-sum thinking, we must recognize when we or others use binary thinking. Zero-sum thinking makes it difficult for people to listen to or work with those with whom they disagree. We all must stop and consider if there are more options than the two presented and expand our minds to the idea that there are more than two options in most situations.

- **Acknowledge one size doesn't fit all:** We are not all standing at the same place in society. Some people may have more of something and less of something else and vice versa. We must acknowledge the ways in which oppression can intersect and operate in institutional, interpersonal, and cultural ways. Therefore we cannot and should not embrace the ideology of one size fits all and universal equality. It hasn't worked in the past and is not working now.

With these core stances in mind, educators can move beyond zero-sum thinking, lean into positive-sum thinking, and dream of an education system that prizes holism for students and educators alike.

Pause and Ponder

Pause and ponder the following questions considering what you've read.

- In what ways does the zero-sum paradigm affect student assessment and grading practices?
- Where do you see zero-sum thinking impacting faculty and staff relationships?
- How does the zero-sum mindset shape the way schools address diversity and inclusion?

TRANSFORMING SCHOOL SYSTEMS FROM THE GROUND UP

One question we get often is, "Where do I start? I can't change the entire system." Or we also hear, "I haven't experienced any type of schooling outside of the status quo. How do I know where to start?" We recommend that folks start by trying different things while embracing abundance thinking. Galksi-De'entkw and Luu-MisMaakskw on the *Free Range Humans* podcast share that education is a colonial structure but it doesn't have to be (Mehta & Allen, 2023). They go on to share that we naturally learn by doing; thus education needs to be a time of doing. They also state that schools often try to take culture and fit it into a colonial education system, yet we need to consider how education naturally fits with us, and that's how learning happens (Mehta & Allen, 2023). Take, for example, Ms. Xenos's attempts at call and response in chapter 1 (page 9). Call and response is a form of oral storytelling that was co-opted by neoliberal educators as a form of classroom management. Doing call and response organically is a cultural practice to invite students' voices and perspectives. It cultivates joy. Holding onto these two principles in conjunction with holism, we can consider how to transform both the purpose of schooling and how schools operate. To do this, we lean into our change framework. Figure 3.4 illustrates our change framework for transforming schools from the ground up.

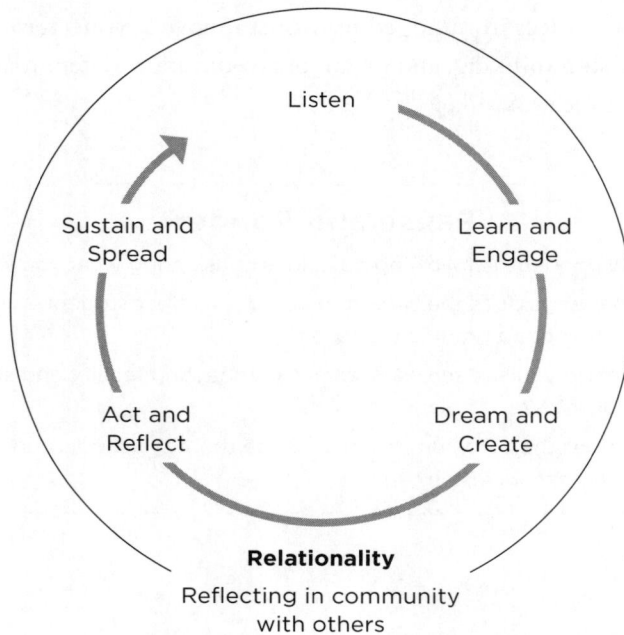

Figure 3.4: Change framework.

To begin, we must listen to and observe other cultures to understand different ways of thinking and working in the world. When we refer to the word *listening*, we don't mean in the Western way of data collection. When we say *listen*, we mean to listen with deep empathy and heart and an openness to learn about other cultures and how they intersect or don't with schooling. To listen, we must transcend the self for a little while and lean into curiosity from a learner's stance.

Then, we must *learn and engage* with others. It is much harder to learn in silos than when we engage each other in discourse. We must learn about and discuss the complex societal problems that often present themselves in our world. We must learn in community with each other if we are going to gain solidarity dividends. Learning in community with others can expand our horizon of thinking and help us unlearn oppressive practices. Our society and school systems purport the:

> Myth that students of color "need developing"—translated: Black, Indigenous, and brown students are broken and schooling will fix them. We must be vulnerable enough to reject this racist lie and stare down the parts of our own practice that need to be fixed. (Safir & Dugan, 2021, p. 52)

We must reflect, learn beyond our horizon, and unlearn the colonial status quo. We must *dream and create* based on the cultural wealth of those who are often marginalized. We must consider how we can create schools that function in ways that are rooted in culture. We must consider what is beyond our purview. Once we dream, then we must act in ways that will transform our system, and reflect on if we still are holding to our core stances as well as consider the impact of the act. Then, we must sustain any positive outcomes so that they can live on beyond one day and become a part of the fabric of the teacher or school. Once you go through this cycle, then you start over by listening.

Undergirding this transformation cycle is the stance that change is more powerful when we reflect in community with others. It recognizes that drawing on the cultural wealth of students is essential to transforming our schools. We do all of this in relationship and community with each other to sustain the change. Figure 3.5 (page 78) illustrates an example of the change framework in action.

Concern: Teachers do not have autonomy in their classroom practice with respect to curricular choices.

Change Attribute	Stakeholders	Action	Guiding Questions
Listen	Include the following stakeholders. • Teachers • Students • District personnel (if applicable) • Legislative personnel	Consider the following action items. • Conduct empathy interviews with all stakeholders. • Conduct quantitative surveys among the staff to assess perception of curricular choices.	Consider the following questions. • What is the root cause of this problem? • Who do we need to have intentional conversations with to learn more about the problem? • What are the common factors contributing to this issue? • What systemwide or policy-based practices are influencing this issue?
Learn and engage	Include the following stakeholders. • Teachers • Students • District personnel (if applicable) • Legislative personnel	Consider the following action items. • Conduct an equity audit of existing curricular practices. • Examine the chain of command related to the approval of particular curricular items. • Include key stakeholders in conversations around findings.	Consider the following questions. • What do we hope to change? • Who is needed to be a part of the decision-making process? • How do we leverage stakeholders to help make change and revisions? • How can we measure impact and success?
Dream and create	Include the following stakeholders. • Teachers • Students • District personnel (if applicable) • Legislative personnel	Consider the following action items. • Analyze the data and trends from the previous steps in the cycle. • Design a theory or action or logic model to support the execution of a plan. • Determine how you are going to measure impact.	Consider the following questions. • What systemic constraints hinder my ability to teach authentically? • How can I navigate these constraints creatively to stay true to my teaching philosophy? • How can I collaborate with colleagues to share and develop authentic teaching practices? • What feedback mechanisms can I put in place to continuously assess and improve my authentic teaching practices?

Concern: Teachers do not have autonomy in their classroom practice with respect to curricular choices.

Change Attribute	Stakeholders	Action	Guiding Questions
Act and reflect	Include the following stakeholders. • Teachers • Students • District personnel (if applicable) • Legislative personnel	Consider the following action items. • Create a common structure or protocol for determining how you will gather data of impact. • Assess and reflect on patterns using a preconstructed protocol. • Determine if the change was impactful or effective as desired.	Consider the following questions. • What have we learned about ourselves in this process? • What additional steps or actions are needed to address the concern? • Who is directly impacted by the results? • What do the results help us to learn or understand?
Sustain and spread	Include the following stakeholders. • Teachers • Students • District personnel (if applicable) • Legislative personnel	Consider the following action items. • Consider best practices from previous adjustments to the system. Modify those that were not as successful. • Ensure adjustments are related to the aspiration authenticity of the teacher(s) in question. • Plan to iterate the idea and loop in stakeholders to ensure continued success.	Consider the following questions. • How do we ensure sustainability of this idea? • How do we ensure that students and teachers are able to maintain authenticity? • What other systemic factors might need to be changed based on the success of this idea?

igure 3.5: Sample change framework.

*isit **go.SolutionTree.com/diversityandequity*** *for a free reproducible version of this figure.*

Consider the Zulu value system: "*Ubuntu* [I am because we are]." In other pan-African cultures, *Ubuntu* can be translated as "humanity toward others." It promotes the value that a person's well-being is intrinsically tied to the well-being of others, and that by working together, we can achieve greater success and happiness. If we all lean into the concept of *ubuntu* as we work toward seeing the system and school change, then we will be one step closer to equity.

SUMMING UP

Throughout this chapter, we focused on how larger systems can influence our identities and the learning spaces we are able to create. Subsequently, zero-sum thinking is pervasive in school systems and influences our perceptions of our role and how we should present ourselves to students.

Consider the following key takeaways from this chapter.

- Educational structures within the United States are representative of a larger system.

- Systems are designed to produce particular outcomes. If systems are steeped in racial ideologies, they will produce racialized results.

- Zero-sum thinking is the belief that one person has to lose for the other to win. In the United States, racialized thinking has resulted in zero-sum systems that are problematic for all people.

- As educators, we have to consider the ways in which systems and structures steeped in racial practices have influenced our perception of schools and schooling practices.

- To transform our systems, we must move away from zero-sum thinking by leaning into abundance, asking questions, valuing culture, and reflecting on our mindsets. And we must acknowledge one size doesn't fit all.

- Educational systems can strip away our identity and authenticity if we do not take the time to unpack and heal from these experiences.

Unpacking Internalized Beliefs

This exercise invites you to examine the systems at work within your educational context, recognize beliefs you've internalized as a result of the culture of these systems, and then consciously dream a new way of being that reforms the system. Consider the following questions associated with each prompt, and write a response in the space provided.

System Name

What system or subsystem do I recognize at play in my educational context?

Internalized Beliefs

What beliefs or stories do I hold that are informed by this system?

How does it appear in my current practice?

Where do these beliefs come from?

In response to these beliefs, am I consciously disrupting oppressive practices or unintentionally perpetuating them?

Dream and Reimagine

If I could reimagine this system, what would it entail?

How does my reimagined version compare to my current practice?

What action can I take to enact this dream?

CHAPTER 4

SCHOOLING, AUTHENTICITY, AND STUDENT RELATIONSHIPS

Many moons ago I, Jacobē, erupted at a student who used the electric pencil sharpener in the middle of my lesson. It was disruptive, it grated my nerves, and it was what felt like the billionth time this student had done the exact same thing and been corrected. The student looked so surprised. Later in the period, I felt bad for my overzealous response and had a one-to-one conversation with the student to discuss what happened and apologize. Still, I felt like a failure and was pretty sure I'd embarrassed the student.

In hindsight, I notice some questions coming up for me.

"What would have happened if this class lesson had been shaped as *our* lesson versus *my* lesson? Would my response have been different?"

"What would have happened if I had taken the time to unpeel the onion of why my student felt the need to move and sharpen the pencil at this moment multiple times?"

"What would have happened if I hadn't thrown around my power as the teacher? What would have happened if I didn't *have* this power to throw around as a teacher? Would I have still dehumanized the student?"

This person is well into adulthood now and we have lost touch, so I don't know how my former student would respond to these questions. But I do know that incidents like this are not rare; they happen frequently in the classroom. Dynamics between teachers and students have to change.

Students are not empty receptacles that teachers blindly pour into. Students have their own needs and desires. In chapter 1 (page 9), we defined authenticity as being in touch with your inner self so you don't get lost in pleasing others in ways that are detrimental to yourself and your students. To be authentic educators, we must consider how the legacies of meritocracy, hidden curriculum, high-stakes testing, and other harmful facets of the education system show up in our teaching. In chapter 3

83

(page 55), we spoke about the various layers of systemic thinking that exist within schooling practices. These layers are interconnected to the legacies of meritocracy, hidden curriculum, and high-stakes testing. These histories often generate tension between teachers and students at the margins as they encourage singular narratives of students, applying labels such as "low," "English learner," "on the spectrum," "lazy," "a problem," and others.

These labels normalize seeing students as objects or commodities that require fixing. This results in tensions of the spirit, mind, and body that can affect how teachers and students interact with one another. Schooling as a system works to remove authenticity. To embody an authentic practice, teachers must shift these teacher-student dynamics. This is contingent on educators doing the crucial work to unpack various attributes of who they are, the beliefs they hold, and elements of socialization that manifest in their pedagogy.

Guiding Questions

In this chapter, we focus on the following questions:

- How do your identity and schooling experiences inform how you see your students?
- How might your lived experiences influence the ways in which you perceive power dynamics in the classroom?
- What is your definition of power?
- What connections exist between your perception of power and instructional practice?
- How can we take strides toward creating a collectivist environment for learning?

SEEING THE SYSTEM

Negative tensions between teachers and students (like the one I shared at the beginning of this chapter) occur daily. Educational culture accepts this as a normal part of teaching. No one wins when relationships or interactions between students and teachers are adversarial or antagonistic. Teachers don't win. Students don't win. Yet, accepting adversarial teacher-student relationships is the status quo in K–12 education (Emdin, 2021). At the root of being authentic and not harming students is getting to know them for who they are. The system of schooling often undermines teachers' ability to create authentic relationships with students. Figure 4.1 shows some of the factors that contribute to the tensions between students and teachers that can erode authenticity.

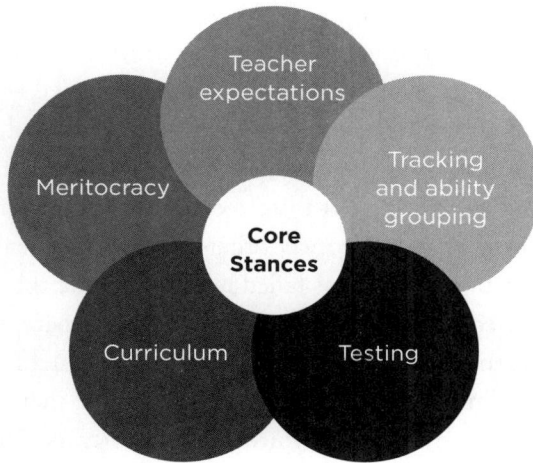

Figure 4.1: Factors contributing to teacher-student tensions.

In chapter 3 (page 55), we discussed how the system is *designed* to produce the current outcomes. Figure 4.1 names the factors contributing to teacher-student tensions. The ideology of *meritocracy* justifies the existing schooling system, which blames students who don't achieve at high levels for their own lack of achievement. The *hidden curriculum* maintains the status quo, creating laborers and bosses, a hierarchy that protects the interests of those at the top. *High-stakes testing* and *ability tracking* further the narrative of underperforming students as "low" or "struggling." These single stories are detrimental to students at the margins and contribute to *teachers' low expectations* for linguistically and culturally diverse students. These factors work together to create the underlying tensions between teachers and students.

To fully see the system that produces the current educational outcomes, we as teachers must consider the historical context that affects the schools and communities in which we teach. This work can be challenging and uncomfortable for teachers, especially those who view systems as "the way it's always been" rather than a structure designed to produce the given outputs. The reality that an unjust system didn't just happen but was constructed that way can be difficult to accept. If teachers hope to participate in changing the system, though, they must do this difficult work of understanding how systems are constructed and recognizing the power each person has to disrupt that system. We as teachers cannot advocate for change by remaining passive participants in existing inequitable structures. In the following sections, we'll take a closer look at each of the five factors contributing to teacher-student tensions.

Hidden Curriculum

The *hidden curriculum* refers to content, topics, or ideologies that purport implicit messaging within larger nation-states that citizens are expected to internalize. In the United States, there is an implicit relationship between the hidden curriculum and its economic system. Capitalism is an economic system that champions individual, private ownership and commerce with limited interference from the government. Liberal education reform prizes the concept that education is the great equalizer; yet, over 150 years of education reform has failed to demonstrate this (Bowles & Gintis, 2011). As you discovered in chapter 3 (page 55), the systematic barrier to transformative education reform is that a capitalist economy produces inequity by design (Au, 2011; Bowles & Gintis, 2011). If we grant the premise that education's purpose in a capitalistic society is to produce future workers (Stivers, 2021), it also stands those workers inevitably fall into one of two categories: laborer or manager. Any such economy will inevitably feature a minority of managers controlling a majority of laborers (Bowles & Gintis, 2011).

Schools that primarily serve students from working-class families tend to center compliance, stricter disciplinary codes, and submit to authority figures (Freire, 1968/2000). This is to prepare workers who will follow the rules and lack agency and democracy in their jobs. Schoolwork in this context tends to look more like following steps or displaying discrete behaviors, such as copying things down; students engage in very little decision making, and the teacher controls time and space without input from students (Anyon, 1980). For example, "This is how you do a two-digit division problem. Show your work at each step. Here are the materials." Students are rarely encouraged to take a critical perspective, employ creativity, or be excited about schoolwork. Conversely, schools that serve students from wealthy families often tend to center creative thinking and prepare students to think systematically or practice making prescriptions for what others should do (Stivers, 2021).

I, Jacobē, experienced this the first time I visited an affluent, majority-White professional school in New York, just after I'd spent time in a working-class, racially Brown school. Three hours into the workday at the affluent school, I hid in the bathroom. I cried, overwhelmed by the waves of emotion rolling over me. I thought about the difference between the two schools. They were both elementary schools within the same larger school system, yet they functioned very differently. In the affluent school, teachers allowed students to get out of their seats to get water; they didn't need to ask for permission. Students moved around the classroom freely to get items from their backpacks or from another classmate. For example, when students needed tissues or water, they just got out of their seats and got what they needed. Conversely, in many of the other schools I work in, students can only get water during certain times of the day or must raise their hands to get out of their seats to get a tissue. I realized during this visit that most of the other schools I worked at were policing Black and Brown students from working-class families in ways I hadn't noticed. Students in the affluent school were given opportunities to reflect and revise their work accordingly and without assumption of capacity. We know these are just two anecdotal examples. However, we have worked in enough schools to see the tangible difference. I wished every school I worked with offered students the same creativity, autonomy, and freedom that students accessed in the affluent school.

The dynamics created by the hidden curriculum are also reflected in research. The following chart draws on the foundational work of Jean Anyon (1980) to demonstrate the progression of how educational experiences can differ. Table 4.1 (page 88) outlines Anyon's findings. As you will see, the "hidden curriculum" of schools is to prepare students for different levels of the workforce (Alsubaie, 2015; Au, 2011; Boston University, n.d.). In her study about her lived experiences, Merfat Ayesh Alsubaie (2015) finds that the hidden curriculum is still alive and well in schools today. As you explore these levels in the table, you will see a difference in what the classroom pedagogy looks like and the outcomes it produces based on socioeconomic levels.

If teachers are going to be authentic and enable great opportunities for the students they serve, they must reflect on the ways in which they participate in and perpetuate this hidden curriculum. Use the reproducible "Recognizing the Hidden Curriculum" at the end of this chapter (page 110) to support this self-reflection.

Navigating authenticity in teaching while meeting structured educational demands creates a challenging balance. On one hand, teaching authentically involves connecting with students through personal values, unique teaching styles, and genuine interactions, fostering a classroom where students feel supported and engaged. On the other hand, the increased focus on performance metrics, standardized curricula, and outcome-based assessments can sometimes feel disconnected from a teacher's philosophy and students' diverse needs. This structure may limit teachers' ability to adapt lessons creatively, pushing them to prioritize compliance over building trust and engagement. Balancing these factors requires a nuanced approach, where teachers carve out space within these frameworks to exercise their unique voice and creativity, aligning both with institutional goals and personal integrity.

Pause and Ponder

Pause and ponder the following questions considering what you've read.

- Which class is most strongly represented in your student population?
- Which class was most strongly represented in the schools you grew up in?
- What examples of the hidden curriculum do you see in your content area or from your own schooling?

Table 4.1: Societal Constructs and the Curriculum

Class	Education	Example	Produces
Working Class	Teachers expect students to: • Adhere to stricter disciplinary codes • Submit to authority figures • Follow steps • Copy things down • Rarely make decisions • Submit to teacher's control of the space and time without providing input • Exhibit little creativity • Ignore critical perspectives	"This is how you do a two-digit division problem. Show your work at each step. Here are the materials."	Education for working-class students produces: • Workers who follow the rules and lack agency • Workers who will likely hold similar jobs as their parents
Middle Class	Teachers expect students to: • Get the right answer and understand how they got it • Follow directions • Occasionally make decisions • Rarely exhibit creativity • Ignore critical perspectives • Adopt ideas from teachers or curriculum rather than expressing their own ideas • Rarely experience excitement for schoolwork	"You can choose to do two-digit division the long way, the short way, or in your head. Tell how you did it and justify your answer."	Education for middle-class students produces: • Workers who will likely hold similar jobs as their parents

	Teachers expect students to:		Education produces:
Affluent Professional	• Complete creative activities independently • Express and apply ideas and concepts • Choose the methods and materials they'll work with • Work independently to complete a product • Negotiate for control of the classroom using students' input • Carry out self-directed learning, needing few direct orders	"Collect data about how many video or board games fifth-grade families have at home. Find the average, compile data, and compare with the fourth-grade class data. Classmates must verify your work."	Education for affluent students produces: • Professionals who prescribe what others should do • Managers
Executive Elite	• Develop analytic powers • Understand how systems work and use that insight to problem solve • Make decisions • Understand that right answers matter but are not given • Challenge answers • Find efficient solutions • Discuss current issues • Complete fewer creative assignments in favor of more "academic" writing • Exhibit self-control • Move freely around the school	"Knowing what we know, can we think of a formula (versus *the* formula) for area?"	Education for elite students produces: • Executives who prescribe what others should do • Owners

Teacher Expectations

Classism and economics are not the only factors that influence the hidden curriculum. A teacher's intersectional identity can impact the lens through which they see the content and curriculum. In chapter 2 (page 25), we discussed the concept of intersectionality. People's lived experiences differ based on the intersection of their identities. Thus, just like class can affect your school experiences, the intersection of your class, race, sex, gender, neurodiversity, or other identity affects your experiences. For teachers, intersectionality factors into the explicit and implicit expectations we have for students and how they present in the school environment. Schools reproduce the societal disparities based on the identity markers (genderism, racism, neurodiversity, sexism, and so on) of their students via differences in teaching methods and philosophies of education.

Table 4.2 provides a high-level view of some of the big ideas that may impact how students experience the classroom, especially in response to the teacher's expectations. This table highlights how the intersectional identities of both teachers and students can influence classroom dynamics and educational outcomes. Teacher expectations play a crucial role in shaping the classroom environment and influencing student engagement. These expectations are intertwined with the teacher's identity and experiences, which can impact how they perceive and interact with their students. Classism and economics are not the only factors that influence the hidden curriculum; a teacher's intersectional identity can also affect their perspective on content and curriculum.

Without an understanding of and appreciation for students' diverse identities, teachers often see students as different from themselves. Additionally, the mismatch in cultures between students and teachers can often stifle learning (Milner, 2003). Many mandated, scripted curricula have reduced the process of getting to know student identities on a deeper level as teachers are no longer prompted to engage in a preliminary level of student investigation.

What happens when students intuit that their intersecting identities don't fulfill their teacher's explicit or implicit expectations? Think of a time when your culture or identity was seen as a deficit rather than an asset. How did that affect you? Now consider what that means for students in environments that chronically deem them inferior. These effects of cultural invasion lead to harm, tensions, or misunderstandings in the classroom.

Table 4.2: Intersecting Identities and Implications for Classrooms

	Big Ideas	**Factors Influencing How Students Are Taught**
Race Matters	• Students don't see themselves in the curriculum. • Black students are more likely to be suspended. • Students of color are more likely to experience "spirit-murder" or practices that reduce, humiliate, and destroy people of color (Love, 2019). • Race and poverty are not synonymous. Teachers must disaggregate data by race to consider who the school is working for and under what conditions.	• Curriculum usually is not a reflection of students' lived experience. • Black students are less likely than White students to access college-ready courses. • Black male preschoolers are more likely to be suspended than their White counterparts (Nittle, 2021). • On average, Black girls experience adultification, overrepresentation in suspensions, and other events that push them out of school (Morris, 2018). • Black and Latino students are more educationally segregated today than they were two decades ago (The Annie E. Casey Foundation, n.d.). • Students of color with the same test scores as White and Asian students are less likely to be placed in advanced classes (The Annie E. Casey Foundation, n.d.). • Because of race and class segregation and its relationship to local school revenue, students in high-poverty racially segregated schools are not exposed to high-quality curricula, highly qualified teachers, or important social networks as often students in wealthier, predominantly White schools (The Annie E. Casey Foundation, n.d.).

continued →

	Big Ideas	Factors Influencing How Students Are Taught
Gender Matters	Gender influences the choices students make and the societal boxes schools try to fit students into.	• Queer and gender-nonconforming youths are significantly overrepresented in the juvenile justice system; and more than 60 percent of the 300,000 gay and transgender youths arrested and detained each year are Black and Latino (Staples, 2019).
Ability Matters	The medical model of education ascribes an abnormal label to neurodiverse and disabled students.	• The history of the eugenics movement colors how schools and society view neurodiversity (Valle & Connor, 2019). • Educators' preconceptions and expectations often perpetuate the marginalization of students with disabilities. • Histories of race and disability in the United States are inseparable—racism validates and reinforces ableism, and vice versa; additionally, society normalizes this dynamic (Annamma, Connor, & Ferri, 2013). Students with this intersectional identity are disproportionately disciplined or expelled.
Class Matters	A student's socioeconomic class affects their experience in school, which determines the kinds of professional opportunities they access.	• The wealthiest 10 percent of U.S. school districts spend nearly ten times more than the poorest 10 percent.
Language Matters	The English language is not intrinsically oppressive, but it has been historically used to silence all other languages that are deemed "inferior" to standard English (hooks, 1994).	• Students who speak White mainstream English are better positioned for achievement than those who don't because their cultural ways of being, their language, their literacies, their values, their histories, and their knowledges are privileged in classrooms (Baker-Bell, 2020). • Black students who are taught to abolish Black speech may internalize the message that they are inferior (Baker-Bell, 2020).

Meritocracy

Meritocracy, the idea that those who are most talented or work the hardest move ahead in life based on their achievement is another factor inherent in status quo education that breeds teacher-student tensions.

You've seen it in action every time a teacher expects a student to pull themselves up by their bootstraps. The term *meritocracy* was coined by British sociologist Michael Young in his 1958 satirical work, *The Rise of the Meritocracy*. Young used the term to criticize a society in which social status and success were determined solely by individual merit and intelligence, leading to a rigid class structure. In the United States, the idea of meritocracy has been present since the early years of the nation, but it gained popularity during the post–World War II era, in the 1950s and 1960s. This period saw an emphasis on education, economic growth, social mobility, and the American Dream, which caused the concept of meritocracy to flourish.

The problematic assumptions embodied in the idea of meritocracy became more prominent as scholars and educators critically examined the outcomes of education systems. While the concept of meritocracy was initially embraced as a means of promoting equal opportunities based on individual abilities, it became evident that various factors, including socioeconomic disparities, systemic biases, and unequal access to resources, undermine the ideals of a purely meritocratic system. The problem with meritocracy is that it assumes everyone has equal power in society. In a society where the purpose of schooling is to maintain the status quo and perpetuate the hierarchical structure, everyone does not have equal power.

Schools and educators participate in the myth of meritocracy every time they use objectivity, fairness, and hard work to justify why some folks are successful and others are not. In this model, the dominant culture sets the criteria for achieving social position. Anyone who doesn't meet the standard—such as neurodiverse and racially diverse students—takes the blame for their underachievement. Unwittingly, educators may approach or interact with students differently if they don't fit the dominant image of the model student (Delpit, 2006; Emdin, 2021).

When I, Jacobē, was teaching seventh grade, I sat in the teacher's lounge and listened to my peers' conversations. They were discussing how one particular student was lazy and slow. Thinking back on the conversation, I wonder how we as teachers had become so comfortable forming opinions of students based on the metric of perceived hard work. In this case, we later found that the student was neurodiverse and needed accommodations to help him process the information. By holding onto these meritocratic ideas, my peers and I unwittingly leaned away from authenticity and into harm. In her recent text, *Unearthing Joy*, Gholdy Muhammad (2023) offers alternative phrases to rethink and recondition our perspective on students. Take, for example, the common phrase "developing skills." This can be swapped with "developing genius." When we become more cognizant of our lexicon when describing students, we humanize their capacity. This humanization pushes us to move away from the notion of which students "deserve" their merits. The simple shift in language can influence how we see our students and assess their worth in class and ultimately in society writ large.

Testing

IQ (intelligence quotient) testing has played a historical role in education with long-lasting effects that still affect the institution today. IQ testing is a method that attempts to assess an individual's cognitive abilities in relation to others. The goal is to measure a person's intellectual potential and predict their performance in various cognitive tasks and evaluate different aspects of their intelligence. NPR's Celeste Headlee (2013) reports that "schools have long used IQ tests and standardized tests of many varieties to group kids and teach each kid according to his or her abilities." The downside, though, is that students move into their education with a label attached to them—one that influences their experience in the classroom and follows them throughout the rest of their education (Headlee, 2013). Not only that, but IQ testing is also part of a troubling legacy in the United States. IQ testing grew out of the eugenics movement of the early 20th century. The eugenics movement pursued race-purifying policies by identifying desirable and undesirable genetic traits that should be controlled through selective breeding. Researcher Ajitha Reddy (2008) explains the movement's connection to IQ testing:

> Throughout the early 1900s, eugenicists labored to devise objective methods of measuring and quantifying valued traits, including intelligence, in order to substantiate their hypothesis of Nordic genetic advantage. . . . Eugenicists struggled for years to produce compelling results, until the advent of Alfred Binet's intelligence scale in 1909 gave rise to standardized intelligence testing, colloquially known as IQ testing.
>
> Armed with this so-called objective methodology, American eugenicists advanced a straw-man rationale for large-scale testing. They reasoned that society needed to identify, segregate, and sterilize the "feeble-minded," initially defined as those with mental disabilities but later extended to include any "unfit" person of low intelligence, character, or ethnicity. (p. 668)

During the 19th and 20th centuries, the movement used IQ tests to justify forced sterilization and medical experimentation on those deemed mentally "unfit" (Stern, 2016). Although the United States no longer sanctions many of the practices common to the eugenics movement—involuntary sterilization, forced institutionalization, social ostracization, and others——IQ tests remain. Unfortunately, IQ tests don't provide an adequate or accurate picture of intelligence. They leave out environmental factors. They don't measure a person's aptitude to grow. They don't account for language factors. And yet they are treated as an authoritative measure of intelligence, which affords them power to denigrate students and label them as inferior to the dominant culture.

Even when IQ tests don't come into play in K–12, the same mindset shows up through screeners and state tests. Educators commonly use state test scores to label students "low-achieving" or to create a singular narrative of students rather than viewing them through the ampleness of their identities or celebrating their assets. Over time this can create an enduring narrative about a student's worth that the student may internalize or teachers may adopt without question. We as educators must reflect on how we use testing in our classrooms and consider whether we are leaning into authenticity or harm.

Tracking and Ability Grouping

Tracking and ability grouping impact teachers' views of students. *Tracking* is any school process in which teachers or administration attempt to homogenize classroom placement of students based on their perceived academic, social, and economic similarities (Darder, 2012). Tracking and ability grouping build the confidence of a select few at the expense of all other students. They socialize students in the lower tracks to see themselves as deserving less from life while those in the higher tracks tend to expect more (Darder, 2012).

Tracking also socializes teachers to categorize students according to their track. The tracking process is heavily dependent on teacher expectations. Oftentimes students in lower-tracked classes don't have the opportunity to access grade-level work. According to Debbie Truong (2022) at *U.S. News and World Report*, tracking disproportionately affects low-income Black and Latinx students and is harmful to lower-tracked classes, as most times they aren't exposed to challenging coursework. Additionally, tracking does not provide any significant benefits to the higher-tracked students.

Most teachers have probably heard students refer to being in the "dumb class." Imagine what kind of messages a student might internalize in that situation. Intersectionality and tracking systems can profoundly impact teacher-student interactions and how students are treated within the educational system. Teachers' expectations, shaped by their own identities and biases, can influence how they perceive and interact with students. Tracking systems and ability grouping can further exacerbate these differences by creating environments where students are treated according to the labels assigned to them, often perpetuating existing inequalities. To foster a more equitable and inclusive classroom, teachers must be aware of these dynamics and strive to recognize and challenge their biases, ensuring all students receive the support and encouragement they need to succeed. We also need to consider the psychological implications of being tracked. There are long-standing consequences of being demoralized with implicit messages associated with intellectual worthiness.

When the education system perpetuates a hidden curriculum, a meritocratic ideology, narratives of students based on tests, inaccurate teacher expectations, and ability grouping, classrooms buzz with low-grade tension. It doesn't take much for conflict to erupt. It is hard for teachers to lean into authenticity. Teachers and students face multiple barriers to connected, cooperative relationships. We must all pause and consider, how are these factors in tension with authenticity?

The result of this conflict is that oftentimes students at the margins are seen as objects or commodities that require fixing. Such a mentality dehumanizes students, invalidates their experience, and marginalizes their brilliance.

What types of tensions arise between teachers and students in the classroom as a result of the factors we've discussed in this chapter? Table 4.3 examines behavioral tensions, mental tensions, and spiritual tensions.

We reflect to be more authentic in ways that don't harm ourselves and others. Take a moment to reflect on what tension between yourself and your students looks like in your classroom. What would you add to the previous table? How do those tensions spark conflict? And how does that experience affect your relationships, your learning environment, your success as a teacher, and the success of your students as learners?

Table 4.3: Overview of Tensions Between Teachers and Students

Common Tensions	Explanation
Behavioral	• Student actions are on the fringe of respectability. • Student actions don't fit dominant cultural norms. • Tensions lead to infractions and consequences in schools. • Teachers and students may verbally argue or strongly disagree with one another. • There is a power struggle between students and teachers.
Mental	• Students may shut down or become bored. • Students may not prioritize school. • Teachers may respond with strong emotions toward a student.
Spiritual	• Teachers' spirits are weakened by a system that overworks, underpays, and treats teachers like factory workers. • Students' spirits may be "murdered" by the impacts of a system that humiliate, reduce, and destroy (Coates, 2015).

TRANSGRESSING AGAINST THE SYSTEM

To move beyond the status quo that hinders authenticity, we as teachers must transgress its boundaries. In *Teaching to Transgress*, bell hooks (1994) posits that educators should use the classroom to defy and push against the current borders of traditional education models as a practice of freedom. hooks (1994) states that we as teachers should "open our minds and hearts so that we can know beyond boundaries of what is acceptable, so that we can think and rethink, so that we can create new visions" (p. 12). If we hope to shift the dynamics of chronic tension between teachers and students, we must transgress against the status quo, disrupt the dynamics that perpetuate those tensions, and create new norms in our classrooms and collaboration with our students. We acknowledge that some teachers work in unsafe environments, perhaps to the point that they can't even discuss the ideas raised in this book. Our intent is not to place you in a precarious situation. The following list offers a series of guiding or affirmation prompts and activities you can consider if you have limited autonomy.

• Offer students input in classroom practices. This can be done through the strategic inclusion of feedback from empathy interviews. Students can also have access to choice boards that all provide them with autonomy in the tasks they choose to complete.

- Provide reciprocal feedback across all aspects of the school system. This will allow for more dreaming and reflection.

- Co-construct classroom routines and paradigms. Students become more invested when they have a say in the expectations.

- Use affirmations for you and the students to validate what you seek for daily instructional and learning experiences.

Rather than living in the reductionist approach to teaching and seeing students, we can partner with students to shift the schooling within the classroom. When students and educators work together to transcend the status quo, the classroom can become a place of play and liberation where students and educators can fully engage their bodies, minds, and souls.

Pause to Reflect

Pause and ponder the following questions considering what you've read.
- What do the tensions between yourself and your students look like in your classroom?
- What is underneath these tensions?
- What can you control in your local context?

Teachers must transgress in their classrooms and in their schools within their locus of control. There are many things in an educator's control. Ultimately, this is a question each teacher must answer for themselves, but let's explore several possibilities in response to the status quo we've examined so far in this chapter.

IMAGINING A NEW WAY

An essential part of disrupting the status quo or divesting from an oppressive system is imagination. If the system you're in is the only one you've ever known, it can be hard to know what to do to enact change in a way that is authentic and genuine. It's tempting to mimic what others are doing or ask experts to tell us what to do. That's not always a problem—it makes sense to learn from successful people—but it can also lead us to become performative or to enact change in ways that aren't genuine or sustainable. What would happen if you gave yourself permission to imagine a new way, if you trusted that guidance could come from within you? When teachers embrace a practice of imagining new, more equitable ways to connect with and relate to their students, authentic action follows.

Writer, activist, and facilitator adrienne maree brown (2017) writes, "We are in an imagination battle" (p. 18). To change the status quo we must imagine, conceive, and act together so that no more students are "spirit-murdered" and so folks aren't tracked into oppressive systems. brown asks what ideas will liberate teachers and students, stating, "The more people that collaborate on [an] ideation, the more people that will be served by the resulting world(s)" (p. 19).

Consider the following ideas to begin a practice of imagination.

- **Daydream:** Go somewhere quiet and free from distractions. Hold in your mind your intention to disrupt the oppression you witness in your district, school, or classroom. And allow yourself to imagine how it might be different.

- **Journal:** Write about your experiences with oppressive education systems, and identify key questions, emotions, and goals. Use this space as a place to imagine possibilities.

- **Discuss:** Meet with a trusted friend or colleague who is committed to creating equity in the classroom. Agree to talk about your experiences with oppressive educational systems with the goal of brainstorming, dreaming, and imagining new possibilities.

- **Sketch:** On a blank piece of paper, imagine and draw what a new possibility looks, sounds, and feels like.

As you regularly engage with your imagination practice, you'll begin to notice what factors are within your control. Set intentions, goals, or action steps around these factors as a way of moving from imagination to action.

DEMOCRATIZING KNOWLEDGE

A capitalist society survives by competition. Economist and author of *Capitalism: Competition, Conflict, Crises* Anwar Shaikh (2016) notes that "competition and conflict are intrinsic features of capitalist societies, inequality is persistent, and booms and busts are recurrent patterns" (as cited in The New School for Social Research, 2016). Competition is the status quo for 21st century U.S. citizens—even in the classroom. While competition may serve economic ends, it doesn't serve human flourishing.

To transcend the status quo, teachers must be willing to decentralize power and democratize knowledge. The Leading Through Learning Playbook (n.d.) names decentralized knowledge ownership as a key equity principle for learning leaders:

> All knowledge is democratic. Learning leaders decentralize knowl-
> edge ownership. They engage all stakeholders, particularly those
> closest to the work, in the generation, consolidation, sharing, and
> application of knowledge. All stakeholders—including staff, stu-
> dents, parents, and community members—have the opportunity to
> not only give input but also meaningfully contribute to decisions
> about which ideas are worth capturing and scaling. Democratic
> participation strengthens knowledge generation and builds buy-in
> and capacity for knowledge application, yielding better and more
> efficient outcomes.

To do this, teachers must be partners with their students rather than being at
odds. Teachers must be unwilling to accept the status quo tension that arises in the
classroom and take the initiative to change the dynamics that create it. They must
create avenues to work through their difficulties rather than engaging in power
struggles.

I versus We. Competition. Battle of the best. Salutatorian. Valedictorian. Top 5
percent. National Merit Scholarship. When we think about the idea of schooling,
we must also think about the explicit and implicit language that tells us (both students and adults) that only the best survive, gain opportunity, and become "something." Outside of collaborative interludes, there is very little to foster the idea of
collectivism in schools.

Collectivism is not socialism or communism; it's an attitude, an intention to
collaborate rather than compete. According to Zaretta Hammond (2015b), collectivism is the interdependence, harmony, and collaborative work that can occur in
classroom spaces where teachers do not position themselves as the sole authority
figure. In her text, *Culturally Responsive Teaching and the Brain*, Hammond (2015a)
has a ranking of industrialized nations and their beliefs as they relate to collectivism.
The United States is one of the last nations on that list. This essentially means that
the education system in North America doesn't prioritize or value collectivism, but
rather prioritizes individualism and hierarchies of power.

By contrast, collectivism argues that teachers are not the center of the classroom.
They're not the single authority passing down knowledge to ignorant students.
The teachers and students work together as a community to co-create their learning. The classroom space is co-constructed to reflect the diverse cultural beliefs
of its members.

Think back to chapter 2 (page 25) and the nuanced understanding of culture that
we outlined. Culture is much more than the superficial elements that we might visibly discern. It goes beyond surface-level attributes such as religion, race, or political
affiliation and includes the way in which we have been socialized to see the world.

Education often socializes educators to see teaching as a power dynamic in which students are recipients of knowledge. The idea that they possess insight or information that can disrupt old patterns of thinking may be foreign and uncommon—but it's true. What would happen if teachers saw students as their collaborators, as unique and insightful people who had something novel and important to contribute? This is what it means to decentralize knowledge. Further, when teachers adjust classroom routines, practices, and instructional methods with this truth in mind, they cultivate collectivism and authenticity.

Figure 4.2 (page 102) offers recommendations for beginning to cultivate a collaborative space for all students.

Figure 4.2 offers a series of suggestions and activities that teachers can undertake to proactively reconsider the three primary domains associated with instructional practice. The key and crucial element is ensuring that students' voices and perspectives are integrated. The guiding question will encourage reflection to ensure execution occurs as we might hope. Crucial to implementing a collaborative learning space is garnering students' insights. Students are not a monolith; their cultures are not carbon copied. Therefore, their ideas are essential and might require teachers to continuously circle back to gain additional insight. This does not mean that teachers should see themselves as beholden to fulfill every student's request or demand. Rather, they should position themselves as investigators who seek to process the route to a collectivist classroom. Figure 4.3 (page 104) outlines the method for restructuring the role of students in the classroom, thereby allowing them to act as collaborators as opposed to passive recipients of knowledge (Neebe & Sikora, 2022).

Most schools that we work with utilize the Danielson Framework to conduct teacher evaluations and reviews. The distinguishing factor between an "effective" teacher and a "highly effective" teacher in most domains rests in the amount of student involvement within the lesson. Figure 4.3 offers an opportunity to consider how you might intentionally and explicitly involve students in your practice. The figure provides baby steps for integrating students' insight into your classroom. The process for intentionally defining a student role is mapped out in a linear fashion, but it is by no means one-directional. In fact, if teachers want to constantly revisit the purpose of student collaboration, they might begin with the last step and move in a different direction. Comfort with this idea and process allows teachers to lean into a sense of candid vulnerability, thereby lending itself to greater classroom authenticity. The greater the authenticity, the more engaged students become. Greater engagement helps to perpetuate further investment, thereby creating an enhanced sense of collectivism.

Pedagogical Domain	Elements	Recommendations	Guiding Questions for Reflection
Learning environment: The physical and emotional space in which instruction occurs on a regular basis	Elements of the learning environment include • General classroom aesthetics • Organization and layout of the room • Positioning of the teacher's desk and various resources for student use and accessibility • Modalities for neurodiverse students	Shift the power dynamic in the learning environment by: • Including decorations that make the space homey and welcoming (for example, curtains, relaxing colors, comfortable seating, and so on); thrifting is a cost-efficient way to do this. • Moving the teacher's desk away from the front or center of the classroom; place it in the rear. • Positioning classroom desks in collaborative formations (U-shaped, groups) • Asking students to provide feedback on the classroom or arrangement • Providing a space for quiet reflection or contemplation • Creating structures where students can provide feedback or insight	Consider the following questions about the learning environment of your classroom. • Would you be comfortable and happy to spend more than eight hours in this space? • Did students have an opportunity to contribute to the classroom design? • How accessible is the classroom to neurodiverse students? • Would you be happy to have your own children and family members learn in this space?

Pedagogical Domain	Elements	Recommendations	Guiding Questions for Reflection
Instruction: The enacting of teaching or pedagogy based on particular content	Elements of instruction include: • Format or flow of the lesson plan • Percentage of teacher talk to student talk • Selection and planning process of the lesson • Implicit and explicit references to the hidden curriculum • Inclusion of other cultural modes of being and thinking	Shift the power dynamic in instruction by: • Creating structures where students can co-teach a lesson with you (Emdin, 2021) • Soliciting feedback from students on a lesson prior to teaching the content • Time checking elements of a lesson to ensure there is minimal teacher talk • Reflecting on how learning is being transmitted and its relevance to other formats (call and response versus lecture)	Consider the following questions about instruction in your classroom. • How much time do you spend providing direct instruction? • How much time do students have to collaborate with each other? • How do students present or share their learning? Who is the recipient of this learning? • How much insight or input do students have in the creation of the curricular content? • Do students show visible signs of engagement in the content? How do you know?
Expectations: The beliefs held by a teacher as it relates to students, the community, and learning	Elements of expectations include: • Identification of explicit or implicit biases around the community and students • Articulation of what students are capable of and subsequent planning • Perception of self as well as student-held perception of the teacher • Perception of teacher identity	Shift the power dynamic in expectations by: • Monitoring and addressing language patterns around student expectations and capabilities • Noticing actions that represent beliefs around the "soft" layers of teaching (socioemotional needs, identity, and so on) • Journaling around classroom teaching experiences and interactions with students • Soliciting feedback to gauge students' perceptions of classroom environments and culture	Consider the following questions about your expectations in your classroom. • How do you feel about your students? Where do these feelings come from? • Are you approachable to your students? Can they come to you if there is something happening outside of the classroom? • What themes do you notice about your sense of self and identity as a teacher? How does this align to the way students might see you? • What is your aspiration as a teacher?

Figure 4.2: Rethinking pedagogy and power.

Step	Action	Guiding Questions

Teacher Reflection	• As the name implies, teachers are engaged in reflection during this phase.
	• Reflection should center on:
	  + Identity and cultural monikers
	  + Beliefs around the teacher's role in education
	  + Current design and process of teaching
		• How do I identify as a person? As an educator?
		• How are my identity markers representative of my upbringing and experiences?
		• How are my classroom practices representative of my beliefs? Lived experiences?
		• What do I aspire to as a teacher? Is my classroom reflective of this aspiration?

Preliminary Background Gathering	• Gather preliminary information on students using available data metrics as well as qualitative tools (Google survey, empathy interviews, and so on). • Record, with consent, class periods in order to note common patterns around teacher-to-student dynamics as well as who truly "owns" the classroom. • Identify common trends in the gathered data and determine the best areas to begin to cultivate collaboration.	• What trends do you notice from the data you have gathered? • Have you spoken to community and family members? What insights were you able to glean from these individuals? • How are students engaging with your content? Is there a sense of investment in the topic?
Visualize a Role	• Determine an initial entry point for cultivating collaboration with students (for example, norms creation, co-teaching, and so on). • Consider the ways in which this role might help to reimagine classroom management. • Map out an outline of the role that specifies the expectations and responsible parties. • Create a timeline for rolling out the role. • Anticipate making revisions to this plan based on student insight and feedback.	• What role do you envision students taking in your classroom? How does this role lean into collectivist beliefs? • How does your tentative plan ensure there is a sharing or equal distribution of power? • What successes can you envision with your tentative plan? What potential failures might present themselves? • What are your aspirations for creating a collaborative classroom? How does this initial plan fit into that?

Step	Action	Guiding Questions
Interview Students	• Determine the students you would like to interview. In smaller class contexts, we recommend interviewing the entire class if feasible. In larger class contexts, we recommend interviewing between seven and ten students. • Preconstruct interview questions, keeping in mind the intended outcome and envisioned role. • Be prepared to reframe or elaborate on previously constructed questions. • Preview your idealized role of student involvement and be prepared to share this information with students.	• What information would you like to gain from your students? • How will the insights provided from your students help to shape your understanding of the role they should have? • What assumptions might you need to check or address? • Which students will you pick for this process? How do these students represent your class demographics as a whole?
Process and Synthesize	• Determine how you would like to summarize the information. Will you create a report? Jot a few shorthand notes? • Determine the audience for sharing your findings. • Reflect on your original goal and vision and make connections to what has been unearthed. • Make relevant and necessary adjustments.	• What did you learn from this process? • Who should be given access to the information you learned? • What adjustments and mindset shifts might you need to engage in based on the findings? • How will these findings make your classroom more collaborative or collective? • How will these findings help to shift the power dynamics of your classroom?
Share and Enact With Students	• Determine how the gathered information will be shared with students. • Be mentally and emotionally open to the feedback students might pose in response to the synthesized feedback. • Ask students to think about the role of this information in determining classroom actions that lend themselves to collectivism. • Create a plan of action with clear benchmarks of accountability for all parties.	• What information should be shared with students? What information should remain within the teacher's knowledge base? • How might students react to the information that is gathered? • How might this impact their perception of the role they would like to play in class?

Figure 4.3: Action steps for adjusting power in the classroom.

ADJUSTING POWER DYNAMICS

I, Reshma, teach several graduate school courses as an adjunct professor. In one of these classes, I overheard several students commenting on whether or not middle school students could be wittier than their teachers. They argued that students don't have superior wit or intellect to their teachers. Teachers are smarter than students.

My students' commentary illuminated a distorted power dynamic. They imagined that one day as teachers, they would be superior because of their position as educators. Their age, experience, and position would separate them from their students. In addition, I sensed fragility in my graduate students' suggestion that students should challenge a teacher's ego, as if that only comes from malice or spite. They didn't seem to consider the possibility that students challenge teachers' egos from unhappiness or a sense of being disrespected.

More often than not, students who challenge a teacher are not staging a personal attack, but rather seeking to express their unhappiness or discomfort with how they're being taught and what they're learning. Sometimes, it's the best tool they've learned for communicating their needs and desire for change (Emdin, 2021). Because teaching is such a deeply personal profession, though, it's easy to perceive challenges from students as an attack against one's ego and sense of self. I got the sense that these preservice teachers weren't ready to learn *from* students. They were seeing their role through the lens of antiquated power dynamics. They would one day be the "owner of the classroom."

Inherent to their belief is that students are meant to act as recipients of knowledge. These noted patterns will have a profound impact on the type of learning experiences they provide to students. Generally speaking, such a superior mentality is not uncommon among novice teachers. There is a sense of wanting to do right by their students as they believe students have accumulated deficits. The perception of doing right is often grounded in seeing themselves as the sole dispensers of knowledge and learning.

While some preservice teachers outgrow this mindset once they enter their careers, some maintain it and accept that tense and harmful relationships with students are acceptable. If teachers intend to cultivate equitable classrooms, they must disrupt this unjust power dynamic. They must cultivate open dialogue with students and be willing to collaborate to construct the learning space together. As they practice this new way of relating to students, teachers can create new paradigms in other areas such as grading, curriculum, and assessment. Table 4.4 offers an overview of each concept and the strategies that allow teachers to collaborate with students and establish equitable power dynamics.

Table 4.4: Adjusting Elements of Classroom Structures for Equitable Dynamics

School Element	Strategies for Co-Constructing With Students
Curriculum is the explicit and implicit knowledge teachers convey to students through instructional materials, such as lesson plans, handouts, learning activities, and so on. Curriculum is not independent of social and political beliefs. It reflects a teacher's or school district's beliefs around learning. For example, a teacher might choose to teach Shakespeare because they believe it is a source of knowledge. However, some students might be disengaged with Shakespeare because they find the content to be irrelevant (Lalor, 2012).	• Gain insight into student learning preferences based on informal or formal surveys and empathy interviews. Use this information to ascertain connections between students' authentic interests and standards. • Keep abreast of popular culture—even if it isn't your thing. Jacobē is a huge fan of a celebrity family whose last name begins with a K. Reshma thinks that they are biters. Either way, they both keep a pulse on popular culture in order to make the content engaging and relevant. • Find connections between students' lives and the curriculum by continuously learning about your students. This becomes easier as you grow authentic relationships with students. • Solicit feedback from students on proposed units of study or facets of the current lesson. This is also a good opportunity to co-construct the content of the unit with students. • Don't hesitate to discard a unit of study because the students are not feeling it. Ask students to help you imagine or restructure the unit of study for greater investment.
Assessment has been misconstrued in recent years (Wiliam, 2018). The original understanding of assessment is essentially a series of tools that are used to gauge what students have learned and how they have learned it. Assessment, in most learning contexts, is referred to as formative and summative in nature (Brookhart, 2013; Ramkellawan-Arteaga, 2020; Wiliam, 2018). Formative learning assessments are meant to be seen as the how and the what of learning. Summative learning assessments are essentially the end product of what students should have learned throughout a course of study or unit.	• Take the time to learn how students feel about assessment. What assessments do they like to take? What format or modality do they prefer (Brookhart, 2013)? • Co-construct assessments or performance tasks with students. This includes but is not limited to the task itself as well as a corresponding rubric. • Create symbiotic assessments. Teachers assess students on their learning, and students assess teachers on their instructional practice. • Reflect on your beliefs about assessments. Is the assessment's purpose to provide a grade or to provide data for the teacher and student to gauge the student's progress and inform future instruction?

continued →

School Element	Strategies for Co-Constructing With Students
Grading is a quantitative system teachers use to evaluate and measure student progress. The American education system relies heavily on grades as a measure of students' worth and value within the classroom context. In recent years, many institutions have pivoted away from grades as a measure of student learning. Grades are often intertwined with formative assessments.	• Reflect on the values you hold or associate with grading. Ask students to unpack and share their own understanding of the purpose of grading and how they have come to see it through their years of schooling (Milner, 2018). • Work with a cohort of students to rethink the grading policy in your classroom or even school context. We recommend: • Determine the purpose or difference between a zero versus 55 for noncomplete or missing assignments; in many schools, 55 is the qualifying grade for failing a class. Explore whether or not there is value to one over the other. • Determine which assignments should be provided a point value as well as the range of said point value. • Explore the idea of mastery grading, especially as it relates to the topics and standards students are covering. • Review what it looks like when students have mastered a standard. • Unpack the elements of a proficient or exemplary mastery of the standard. Share this information with students beforehand.

Pause and Ponder

Pause and ponder the following questions considering what you've read.

- Name one thing you are willing to try from this chapter.
- Name one action you'll commit to take based on what you've read.
- Name one aspect of this work you're uncomfortable with that you'd like to continue to explore.

SUMMING UP

It's tempting to believe that the challenges and harm teachers and students experience in the classroom result from a broken education system. However, president emeritus of the Carnegie Foundation for the Advancement of Teaching Anthony S. Bryk and colleagues Louis M. Gomez, Alicia Grunow, and Paul G. LeMahieu (2015) frequently remind educators that systems are designed to do what they do. Classrooms are structured to create the dynamics we have explored throughout this chapter. Teachers don't have to accept this as the way it is. They have the power to disrupt inequitable systems through reflection and authentic action. As they imagine a new way, democratize knowledge, cultivate collectivism, and disrupt unjust power dynamics, teachers create supportive and sustainable relationships with their students. Tension and conflict recede, and students and teachers connect in authentic ways to collaborate and co-create equitable learning environments.

Consider the following key takeaways from this chapter.

- Schooling as a system removes authenticity.

- The education system perpetuates a hidden curriculum, a meritocratic ideology, narratives of students based on tests, inaccurate teacher expectations, and ability grouping, all of which can erode teacher-student relationships.

- Common tensions between students and teachers are behavioral, mental, and spiritual.

- To move beyond these problematic practices that hinder authenticity, we must transgress.

- We must actively work to change the tensions in our schools and classrooms. We must partner with our students to do so.

- Rethinking pedagogy and power in our curriculum, pedagogy, instruction, and expectations is crucial to being authentic. When teachers adjust classroom routines, practices, and instructional methods with this truth in mind, they cultivate collectivism.

Recognizing the Hidden Curriculum

In the space provided, journal your responses to the following prompts.

Where do you see the hidden curriculum at work in your school?

In what ways do you observe yourself holding unspoken and inequitable expectations for your students?

What opportunities exist within your locus of control to disrupt elements of the hidden curriculum?

CHAPTER 5

(TRY TO) DO NO HARM

It was my, Jacobē's, first year teaching a new grade. State testing season was upon me. In a staff meeting, my principal outlined the state test preparation plan we must follow for the next two months. Every instructional day, I was supposed to give students an old state test passage. They'd read it, then answer questions, and we'd go over it as a class. Boring! I decided this was not what was best for my students, so I dropped the test prep and continued to teach rich, complex texts and embed skills like close reading and multiple-choice practice.

My students were asked to take a mock state test during eighth period with a brand-new teacher. The average score was 8 percent, though most students didn't even attempt the test. After receiving these results, my assistant principal came into my classroom every day, sitting in the back of the room and scribbling notes the whole time. He made it clear this would continue until my instruction conformed to the test prep plan. I felt like I was walking on eggshells with a target on my back. I knew this is usually the first step in trying to make a case to push a teacher out of the school. I had knots in my stomach each day.

I felt like I was being policed and harassed. I couldn't take it. I finally asked my assistant principal if I was doing something wrong because until that point I hadn't been observed all year, but now I was being observed every day. He said it was because my students all failed the mock state test. I knew my students didn't even attempt to take the mock test, which is why the scores came in so low. I mentioned this and the fact that if the plan the school provided worked, our results would showcase this. On the real state test, the school's average proficiency rate was 23 percent. My students' proficiency rate that year was 60 percent. I stood firm in what I believed was best for my students. Yet at what cost?

Unfortunately in this example, the well-intentioned assistant principal who wanted to ensure students test well created harm for both Jacobē and her students. Pushing a testing-centered curriculum or policing a teacher's instruction may originate with good intentions, yet they contribute to a person's experience of trauma.

In Jacobē's example, the assistant principal wanted students to succeed, so he implemented a testing program dictated by both the overt and subtle systems mentioned in chapter 3 (page 55). He then reinforced these systems and social conditioning through his interactions with Jacobē.

Within the educational sphere, the process of socialization, as discussed in chapter 2 (page 25), can unwittingly become a vehicle for the unintentional perpetuation of harm. Our prescribed roles inevitably conflict with one another. If we don't consciously examine these roles, we perpetuate them and inflict harm on others. To break the cycle and lean into authenticity, we must consider the roles we've internalized, examine the harm they cause, and choose to adopt new roles that place us in constructive relationships with others.

How does social conditioning affect the way teachers view and think about their students? Based on Harro's (2000) cycle of socialization (see figure 2.1, page 26), teachers engage their students and classrooms through a lens in alignment with their identities, experiences, and worldviews. Without committing to a practice of continuous self-reflection, we as teachers can unwittingly cause harm to students. Harm, if unchecked or internalized, can flare up and overflow to others. After all, we know the adage: "Hurt people hurt people. Broken people break people." This is a painful reality to accept. But when we recognize that we have experienced harm, we can interrupt it rather than perpetuate it.

As students and educators navigate the complexities of the school environment, they absorb not only academic knowledge but also societal norms, biases, and power dynamics. These socialization processes can instill implicit biases, reinforce stereotypes, and inadvertently contribute to the creation of harmful narratives. Students and teachers alike may internalize prejudiced perspectives, consciously or unconsciously perpetuating biases that can marginalize certain groups or individuals. Understanding how the educational system can be a breeding ground for unintentional harm is crucial for fostering environments that promote awareness, inclusivity, and conscious efforts to counteract ingrained biases.

In this chapter, we explore how harm can hurt both teachers and students and become a barrier to being authentic. For us to be authentic educators, we must reflect on, work through, and heal our harm and trauma.

Guiding Questions

In this chapter, we focus on the following questions:

- What harm have you experienced in your learning environments?
- How have you responded to the harm you've experienced?
- How have you unintentionally harmed students?
- What is the relationship between acknowledging harm you've experienced and choosing to become an anti-racist, authentic educator?
- How have your beliefs about who deserves to learn influenced the instruction you provide?
- How do you respond to students whose identities challenge your worldview?

DEFINING AND UNDERSTANDING HARM

When you hear the word *harm*, you may think of someone inflicting physical pain on another person's body. Harm does come in this form, but when we talk about harm in an educational context, it often involves more subtle experiences. Take, for example, microaggressions. *Microaggressions* are comments or actions made by people that are grounded in bias or ignorance (Azevedo, 2018). A teacher uttering the phrase, "I don't see color," is a subtle form of harm as it diminishes the student's experiences that are grounded in race. While the teacher meant no harm in making the statement, the impact is quite the opposite for students.

In the context of this book, we define *harm* as an event or series of events that result in trauma. Harm may be enacted through physical, verbal, or psychological means and can be either conscious or unconscious in nature (Menakem, 2017). We see harm in the school context falling within six categories: (1) spiritual, (2) pedagogical, (3) curricular, (4) social, (5) cultural, and (6) neurodiverse. Table 5.1 (page 114) explores these categories in more detail.

It's disturbing to think about the many ways students may experience harm in schools. However, we as teachers don't have to accept this as unavoidable or inevitable. When we see that harm isn't an isolated or random occurrence—it grows, evolves, and may be projected onto others—we can act to stop it. Figure 5.1 (page 117) depicts harm as a process that may be interrupted rather than an endless cycle that can't be broken.

Table 5.1: Harm in Schooling Contexts

Category	Definition	Examples	Reason for Occurrence	Solutions
Spiritual	Spiritual harm may be defined as follows. • This is not necessarily religious but rather a consideration of one's soul. • The soul or spirit is the person. • This is referencing the essence of who the person is and how they exist within the larger schooling system.	Spiritual harm is an attempt to diminish the essence of the person. Examples include: • Assimilation of Indigenous people by missionary schools. • Forced code-switching on students • The need for the CROWN (Creating a Respectful and Open World for Natural Hair) Act or similar legislation	There are a number of reasons for its occurrence, but we believe there is a reinforcing or positioning of one way of being as the best or better than others. This involves: • Enforcement of a scarcity mindset where only certain individuals can "survive" • Limited exposure to other ways of being • Othering different ways of showing up and being present	There are a few solutions to spiritual harm, but they ultimately begin with self-reflection, self-work, and a mindset shift. • Engage in conversation with students or individuals who have different personas than you. Ask why and seek to understand what has made them who they are. • Get uncomfortable with personalities that are different from your own. Investigate why these personas might cause you discomfort.
Pedagogical	The process of inflicting harm through teaching and learning includes: • Punishment and reward systems • Instructional practice • Nonrapport between students and educators • Dehumanization of all educators and students	The examples of harm can be implicit or explicit, depending on the educator or system in question: • Assuming the worst about students through deficit-based language. • Using only one method for learning. • Refusing to include students' cultures or identity. • Centering English-only instruction for multilingual learners.	Pedagogical harm can rest primarily on the teacher's shoulders, but can also be reflective of the larger system—for example: • Teachers' perception of the students and community (see chapter 4, page 83) • Assumptions around the value of education • Uncertainty about how to connect with students	Educators might be limited in the interventions they can include in order to address the pedagogical harm. We recommend the following. • Host informal lunches to build relationships. • Conduct empathy interviews or cogenerative dialogues (Emdin, 2016). • Co-teach a lesson with students. • Ascertain daily feedback on a lesson's effectiveness.

Category	Definition	Examples	Reason for Occurrence	Solutions
Curricular	This particular harm refers explicitly to the documents and lessons used by teachers to provide instruction to students. For example: • Lack of joy or joyous content • Content grounded in White dominant culture or supremacy • Implicit messaging around what is valued (for example, Whiteness) • Nonresponsiveness or stagnancy in the instructional process	The following are several content-specific examples of harm: • Teaching to a standardized test, only • The literary canon • Refusing to include scientists or mathematicians of color in the curriculum • Prioritizing skills and content without cultural content or context	As we see with national movements around critical race theory, curricular harm can come from a number of sources. • This is reflective of a teacher or district's beliefs around the purpose of schooling. • It often resides in schools' and educators' desire to help students "succeed." Success looks different for every one person, however, and depends on one's experiences.	Conduct a curriculum audit to reflect on the inclusion of different voices and perspectives. • Ask students for feedback. • Contextualize curriculum within the community.
Social	Social harm refers to the numerous variables that contribute to our position within the larger society. It is inclusive of: • White constructs of classism • Economics • Race • Schooling • Harm is typically manifested through othering or marginalization	Examples of harm related to socioeconomic contexts include: • One's family is working class, but the individual attends an upper-class private college; they feel a pressure to conform or be labeled as "less than." • A school has explicit policies around articles of dress that include hairstyling.	Reasons for social harm can often be difficult to determine because the context ultimately varies. However, in most situations, it is done to maintain control over particular populations while emphasizing the status quo.	Solutions to social harm can be difficult to manage, when there are other variables that can impede progress (for example, legislation, governing bodies, and so on). However, the following are possible solutions within schooling contexts: • Celebration of different modes of thinking, being, or existence (for example, troubling structures in non-White nations). • Evening economic-related conditions or circumstances (for example, school uniforms, parent-teacher organizations providing funding for school trips, and so on).

continued →

Category	Definition	Examples	Reason for Occurrence	Solutions
Cultural	Cultural harm is the diminishing of cultural beliefs through othering or marginalization. This typically is done when seeking to center White and Western practices as superior or worthy. For specific details related to the definition of culture, we encourage you to reference chapter 3 (page 55).	Cultural harm can occur in a number of ways: • Commodification of Black language or culture (Baker-Bell, 2020). Think the use of Black slang for monetary purposes • Tokenism of cultures and religion (for example, White yoga teachers) • Ignoring the correct pronunciation or spelling of a name	We want to assume that cultural harm comes from a place of unconscious ignorance rather than willful harm. When this is the case, it is of a result of • One's locus of knowledge being limited to specific modes of thinking • Socialization and exposure to other ideas • Discomfort with unfamiliar practices, ideas, or beliefs	We believe that many of the solutions to cultural harm, such as the following, are similar to the solutions to spiritual harm given that cultures contribute to the essence of spirituality. • Name what you don't know and what you seek to learn. • Probe the root of discomfort. Is the discomfort due to fear, humiliation, or contradiction with socialized beliefs? • Act as an anthropologist and seek to acquire new learning and information.
Neurodiverse	Neurodiversity (Sousa & Tomlinson, 2018) refers to individuals who have differing modes of thinking or physical existence. This troubles the language of ableism and encourages the inclusion of nontypical ways of thinking, being, and varying modalities of learning.	There are a number of ways in which neurodiverse harm occurs. This often depends on the type of neurodiversity that exists in the individual. Here are a few examples: • Assuming one's inability or lack of readiness based on traditional modes of assessment • Unintentionally denying access to alternate modes of learning or processing	Sources of neurodiverse harm typically stem from unintentional ignorance. It is based on limited exposure or school systems being hostile to alternative modes of being. These include: • Having a desire for students to learn or process information in a common manner • Not having resources to appropriately differentiate • Othering the individual due to their neurodiversity and assuming it is their inherent fault	Solutions to neurodiverse harm are both technical and adaptive in nature. For example: • Shifting in mindset around what constitute "valid" forms of learning and existence. • Support for more resources and information around how to support neurodiverse learners (for example, modified planning, alternate assessments, and so on).

1. **Roots of Harm:** The underlying or unconcious ways in which harm lives in me.

2. **Perpetuation of Harm:** Circumstances or scenarios that explicitly or implicitly allows harm to manifest in my practice.

3. **Manifestation:** The ways in which lived harm exists in my classroom and other ways of being.

4. **Stop, Reflect and Act:** The cessation of allowing harm to exist by stopping to reflect and adjusting behaviors.

Figure 5.1: The roots of harm.

This graphic calls for a moment of reflection. It asks that we reflect on the way harm lives inside us and the situations that cause this harm to grow or continue in ways that might show up in our teaching practice. Through reflection, we can stop how this harm might be impacting others by adjusting our thinking and behaviors. Figure 5.2 (page 117) contains a self-reflection exercise using the roots of harm framework.

Think of one way you experienced harm as a student in school. Read the following prompts and write your response in the space provided.

Roots of harm: What was the catalyst or original event? Identify the origin of the harm you experienced. Beginning at the root, work your way through each step represented in the figure and consider: (1) How have you been harmed? (2) What life circumstances perpetuate the experience or trigger the memory of the original event? (3) What thoughts, actions, mindsets, or beliefs manifest the underlying harm? (4) What practices do you commit to (reflecting, processing, interrupting, apologizing, adjusting, and so on) that release the underlying harm?

I remember receiving a paper back from my high school English teacher that was covered in red ink. I felt deflated and like a failure. It harmed my self-esteem surrounding my writing ability.

Perpetuation of harm: What life circumstances perpetuate the experience or trigger the memory of the original event?

Any time I enter a new writing situation, I get anxiety about whether I am good enough or can meet expectations for writing.

Manifestation: What thoughts, actions, mindsets, or beliefs manifest the underlying harm?

That I'm not good enough.

Stop, reflect, and act: What practices do you commit to (reflecting, processing, interrupting, apologizing, adjusting, and so on) that release the underlying harm?

I commit to saying positive affirmations about my writing. I commit to interrupting my self-doubt with memories of my writing success. I commit to not tearing up a student's paper in the way I experienced from my teacher so I don't repeat this harm.

Figure 5.2: Reflecting on the roots of harm.

*Visit **go.SolutionTree.com/diversityandequity** for a free reproducible version of this figure.*

As an educator, reflecting on the harm we've encountered as a student or teacher is crucial because we may unconsciously transfer this harm to others. Using the reflection in figure 5.2 as an example, a teacher who was conditioned to be tough by their experience in the classroom might grade a student's work harshly, thinking their students need that experience to become tough. Yet, through reflection, it is possible to foster empathy for self and others. Through introspection we can gain insights into avoiding harmful practices, thus promoting personal growth that informs and enhances our teaching practice.

Additional strategies for reflection include the following.

- Use a journal to store your thoughts.
- Create voice notes or memos in conversation with yourself.
- Engage in a guided meditation focused on releasing trauma.
- Write a letter to your past self.
- Write a letter to the person who harmed you or who you might have harmed.

The practice of self-reflection, processing past harm, and making a conscious choice to adjust behavior are essential first steps. We as teachers must do this work *before* we seek to implement solutions. If we fail to do this necessary work first, we continue to act from the root, perpetuating harm (even if unintentionally). If we are committed to interrupting harm rather than projecting it, we must begin with self-reflection and processing past harm. The first step in processing harm is to name and acknowledge the harm.

Pause and Ponder

Pause and ponder the following questions considering what you've read.

- What harm shows up most in your life?
- What do you do, daily, to address it?
- Does it impact your students? Why or why not?

ACKNOWLEDGING AND WORKING THROUGH HARM

We must reconcile harm to be an authentic educator. Why? What does personal and collective harm have to do with bringing our best self to the classroom? Psychotherapist and author Resmaa Menakem (2017) explains that the pain each person carries in their body affects how they engage the world around them—either by transforming pain in positive ways or by transferring it in negative ways. Menakem (2017) uses the language of *clean pain* and *dirty pain* to describe this phenomenon:

> *Clean pain* is pain that mends and can build your capacity for growth. It's the pain you experience when you know exactly what you need to say or do; when you really, really don't want to say or do it; and when you do it anyway. . . . Experiencing clean pain enables us to engage our integrity and tap into our body's inherent resilience and coherence, in a way that dirty pain does not. Paradoxically, only by walking into pain or discomfort—experiencing it, moving through it, and metabolizing it—can we grow. It's how the human body works.

> Clean pain hurts like hell. But it enables our bodies to grow through our difficulties, develop nuanced skills, and mend our trauma. . . . The body can settle; more room for growth is created in its nervous system; and the self becomes freer and more capable, because it now has access to energy that was previously protected, bound, and constricted. . . .

Dirty pain is the pain of avoidance, blame, and denial. When people respond from their most wounded parts, become cruel or violent, or physically or emotionally run away, they experience dirty pain. They also create more of it for themselves and others. (p. 20)

As human beings who carry hurt in their bodies, teachers are not exempt from this phenomenon. Each of us must come to terms with the reality that our past hurts manifest in our classroom and affect our interactions with students. To become an authentic educator, we must confront the pain we've experienced and the pain we've caused.

Processing past harm is a skill like any other—it may feel unfamiliar at first, but it gets easier with practice. Consider the following tips for developing a practice of acknowledging and processing harm.

- **Acknowledge harm:** Perhaps a memory surfaces, an event triggers an underlying trauma, or a student's behavior touches a nerve. Whatever incites you to remember harm you've experienced, pause and name the harm (for example, use compassionate self-talk, discuss it with a trusted friend, write it down, and so on).

- **Sit with discomfort:** Remembering, witnessing, and naming past harm can be uncomfortable—especially at the beginning of a practice. Practice being with whatever discomfort arises and witness it without judgment. Remember that feelings don't last; when we witness them, they will resolve.

- **Notice resistance:** It can be tempting to resist, bypass, or deny discomfort or pain that arises with this practice, but that only prolongs the pain, allowing it to remain and pass to others. Notice resistance, acknowledge it, stay in it, process it, and allow it to pass.

- **Release the harm:** As you process the harm you've experienced and the feelings that accompany the memory, practice releasing them. There are many ways to do this, such as journaling, meditating, visualizing, speaking with a professional, moving your body, being with a trusted friend, creating a ritual, and so on. If you're not sure how to start, choose an activity that feels comfortable and accessible. As you continue to practice, you'll develop a process that is unique to you.

- **Choose a response:** As we release harm—once our past harms are no longer driving our beliefs, thoughts, and actions—we adjust our actions from a place of conscious, empowered choice. Notice how your thoughts, actions, and responses are different on the other side of processing past harm.

One of Jacobē's biggest learnings from a meditation series she attended is that trauma lives in the body. She learned to hone in on the emotion she is feeling, reflect on how her body feels at that moment, and move through it. With the help of a meditation teacher, Jacobē focused on an experience that was hurtful, in this case, the actions of coworkers making her feel marginalized. After describing the event to her meditation teacher, she was prompted to consider how she felt in her body. She recognized that her heart rate was elevated, and she felt like something was sitting on her chest. She sat in this feeling of discomfort. She was asked to focus in on it and then reflect on what came to mind. She discussed what came to mind with her meditation teacher, who then led her in meditation to finish releasing the harm. After participating in this meditation, Jacobē felt lighter and chose not to let this experience be the prevailing thought in her mind.

If you need a bit more structure to help you begin this practice, use the "Processing Harm and Moving Forward" reproducible (page 139).

INTERRUPTING THE CYCLE OF HARM

Harm lives in each person; teachers must practice self-reflection to process and release past harm if they hope to be in supportive rather than harmful relationships with students. The next step of that work is to widen the circle from the personal to the systemic level. The inevitable outgrowth of our personal work to uproot harm in ourselves is to uproot harm in the systems in which we participate. For teachers, this means noticing harm in our schools, districts, and national structures and working to understand the origin of these harmful dynamics. In chapter 3 (page 55), we discussed the adage that systems do what they are designed to do. We must zoom out and reflect on the ways in which we might support a system as well as how we might work toward disrupting it.

This is key for teachers committed to anti-racist practice to acknowledge that racism doesn't happen in isolation, but is rooted in a system's history. Linda Darling-Hammond's (1998) seminal piece for the Brookings Institution describes the deep relationship between housing inequality, economic access, and educational outcomes. At the intersection of these three roads is the fact that schools that have been historically disenfranchised by White flight or economic policies are typically home to students of color. This is not to say that White students don't face economic hardship in rural schools (Ingersoll & Tran, 2023). The point here is that teacher turnover is highest in both rural and urban districts with high levels of students of color. This turnover makes it hard to close the academic opportunity gap. This practice further perpetuates academic disenfranchisement, diminished resources, and the portrayal of particular schools or communities as undesirable.

If we are getting a bit more granular, let's explore examples of anti-Blackness within the school building itself. When we think about anti-Blackness, the images that might immediately spring to mind are the Ku Klux Klan, segregated fountains, and other explicit examples. But anti-Blackness also shows up more subtly, such as policing the language used by Black people if it isn't White English (Baker-Bell, 2020). Some English teachers in particular love to describe themselves as grammar Nazis. We can attest that such language is heavily prevalent in schools with Black or Brown students, and teachers pride themselves on correcting students' rhetorical patterns. Some schools utilize restorative justice circles among students only, as opposed to having teachers participate in these conversations as a means to remedy interpersonal strife. Finally, anti-Blackness in education is cutting off a young man's locs before a wrestling match (Stubbs, 2019). Many states have passed what is known as the CROWN Act, which protects Black people's right to keep their natural hair, in response, but we must note that such legislation does not even need to exist for other racial groups.

In *Stamped From the Beginning*, author, professor, and activist Ibram X. Kendi (2023) presents the idea of *uplift suasion*. Essentially, if one works hard enough and engages in assimilation, one will achieve success. This idea is pervasive in schools, where it manifests through instructional practices. The use of White-English-only practices, emphasis on code-switching, and policing of students' appearance are all examples of instructional anti-Blackness that perpetuates uplift suasion. Many teachers believe they are helping to "save" students by teaching them to align their behaviors to White norms. Charter schools in particular use the rhetoric of "working hard" as a means for advancing one's status in life. Yet, the ideology associated with uplift suasion fails to account for a larger system and society that maintains racism in its operation principles. For example, KIPP (the Knowledge Is Power Program), a national network of public charter schools, chose to retire its famous "Work Hard. Be Nice." slogan as it supports the myth of meritocracy and ignores the significant challenge that the system can pose (Pondiscio, 2022).

We have outlined the various harms that are culpable in schooling systems. At the core of many of these experiences are racist ideologies that perpetuate zero-sum thinking (McGhee, 2021). Within schooling contexts, this is often presented as the diversion of resources from one school district to another or the subtle push to remove affirmative action as a great equalizer.

Becoming an authentic and potentially activist educator means changing your mind *and* taking action. After all, "an activist produces power and policy change, not mental change" (Kendi, 2019, p. 209). Teachers have the power and responsibility to remedy harm in the classroom. Educational systemic harm can be addressed through greater policy shifts that encourage evolutionary thinking and movement away from decisions that are couched in fear. For example, if there were fewer top-down approaches to education innovation, this would allow teachers and students to determine what initiatives or ideas work for their contexts. If we committed to not using standardized assessments as the only measure of students' and schools' worth, then it would open the opportunity for us to experiment with other means of teaching and learning.

We are conditioned, often through harmful interactions, to internalize problematic ideologies and manifest the associated behaviors when interacting with students. If not attended to, harm limits our authenticity and creates conditions that don't break the cycle. Figure 5.3 offers a visual representation of how harm can exist both within us and within the larger system. Note the parasitic relationship between the harm that anti-Black systems cause and the ways in which we might consciously or unconsciously uphold these practices. This ultimately results in continued harm for all.

Harm at the Root

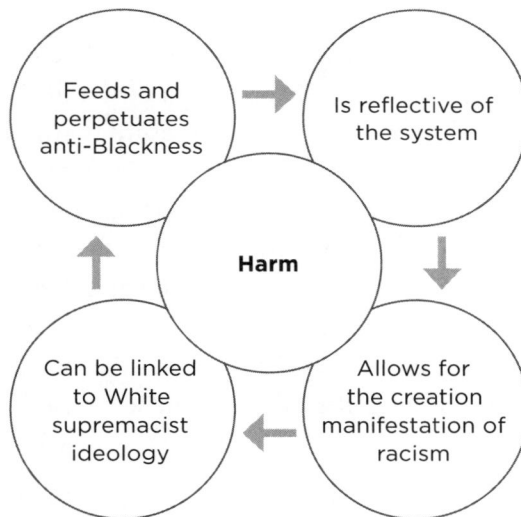

Figure 5.3: Various sources of harm.

Anti-Blackness harm is cyclical if not interrupted. It is held in place by White supremacist ideology and spread through institutions, people, and policy, which can create a fertile ground for racism to manifest. To become authentic educators, we must lean into transformative justice.

Pause and Ponder

Pause and ponder the following questions considering what you've read.

- In what ways have you unintentionally enacted racial and bias-based violence on your students, from an educator-savior perspective?
- How have you engaged in behaviors that stem from your socialized experiences?
- In what ways do you view the parallels between your and your students' experiences as a monolith?

BECOMING AUTHENTIC AND PRACTICING TRANSFORMATIVE JUSTICE

Cultural understanding is foundational to addressing harm through an authentic lens. In chapter 2 (page 25), we discussed how culture impacts our identity. Additionally, Menakem (2017) states, "Culture is how our bodies retain and reenact history through the stories and things that we hold dear and the ways we see the world" (p. 245). Thus, each school has its own culture that retains and reenacts the history of those who occupy its space. Embedded in school culture is a history of political and economic struggles (for example, segregation, high-stakes testing, removal of technical classes, and so on) that consequently lead to harm. Angela Y. Davis (2012) states, "[Histories] are part of us; they inhabit us and we inhabit them even when we are not aware of this relationship to history" (p. 169). Antonia Darder (2012) posits that there has been an overwhelming number of educational practices that have perpetuated harm through the culture of the school and silenced the voices of those most marginalized.

Intentional activism is necessary to bring about change in schools and to heal the legacy of schools being a site of struggle and harm. To collectively heal across our intersectional identities as both teachers and students and move toward humanizing schools and learning spaces, we must create cultural shifts. We must create new expressions of culture that call out and reject oppressive practices (Menakem, 2017). This activism work is not easy, but it is necessary for you to be an authentic teacher who is in touch with your inner self, history, and culture in service of not causing harm or being detrimental to yourself and your students. Menakem (2017) explains as follows:

Social activism is necessary for changing the world in positive ways. But if our collective body is to fully heal from the trauma of white-body supremacy, we must create cultural shifts as well. White-body supremacy is already a part of American culture—in the norms we follow, the assumptions we make, the language we speak, the water we drink, and the air we breathe. This is the case no matter the color of our skin. This means we must create new expressions of culture that call out, reject, and undermine white-body supremacy. This won't be quick or easy—but there is no other way. (pp. 246–247)

To change school culture, we must reconcile harm. Maisha T. Winn (2018) writes about ensuring justice on both sides, which "refers to how students perceive relationships between students and teachers" (p. 26) and vice versa. Scholar and restorative justice practitioner Winn calls educators to embrace a paradigm shift away from asserting authority and harmful power over students to reconciling harm. She states, "The restorative justice circle provides a forum for exploring histories, futures, tensions, and paths forward. In such a process, educators and the students they serve no longer assume oppositional 'sides'; indeed, restorative justice seeks to undermine such binaries" (Winn, 2018, pp. 26–27). The objective of restorative or transformative justice is to build community and cultivate relationships among a group of stakeholders. It is about equity, understanding context, and true accountability, in which everyone acknowledges their responsibility to humanity and makes a commitment to putting things right when they have caused harm (Winn, 2018).

As educators, we need to move away from this "us versus them" mentality when interacting with students. Rather than asserting authority over students, a restorative or transformational worldview requires us to have the mindset to learn how to "be in relationship with students and establish mutual respect and accountability. Accountability is not solely the responsibility of students; educators, too, must be held accountable for their actions and interactions with students" (Winn, 2018, p. 24).

Winn (2018, 2021) posits that educators dedicated to restorative justice must acknowledge five pedagogical stances: (1) race matters, (2) history matters, (3) justice matters, (4) language matters, and (5) futures matter. For the purposes of this book, we include a sixth stance: mindset matters. Figure 5.4 (page 126) provides an overview of the six stances as well as reflection questions that may open doors for you to see a situation differently.

Transformative Justice Stances	Big Ideas	Reflection Questions
History Matters	Taking a pedagogical stance that history matters includes the following big ideas. • "Requires educators to seek out histories that make us uncomfortable and forces us to look critically at the group-level power dynamics that characterize our schools and communities" (Winn, 2018, p. 33). • Teachers must know historical wrongdoings to be able to collectively address historical wrongdoings.	Adopting this stance raises the following questions. • In the past, how have both race and power dynamics been present in your local context? • In the past, what tensions have politicians felt in your local context? • Historically, what issues are raised in conversations among parents?
Race Matters	Taking a pedagogical stance that race matters includes the following big ideas. • "Race matters is informed by history and requires teachers to consider the role of racism and racist ideas in how they think about students as learners" (Winn, 2018, p. 35). • Being unaware of racism does not erase its impact.	Adopting this stance raises the following questions. • What is the role race may play in how you think about your students? • What were you socialized to think about people of different races and ethnicities? • How does race show up in your school?
Justice Matters	Taking a pedagogical stance that justice matters includes the following big ideas. • "Imagine a world where everyone—irrespective of race, ethnicity, socioeconomic status, gender, sexuality, or ability—is able to live with dignity and is recognized as belonging" (Winn, 2018, p. 36). • Embodies the importance of keeping justice as the why behind, and at the forefront of, this ongoing school transformation work.	Adopting this stance raises the following questions. • How might freedom for all show up in your classroom? • How do you currently pursue justice? • What does justice look and sound like in your current context?

Transformative Justice Stances	Big Ideas	Reflection Questions
Language Matters	Taking a pedagogical stance that language matters includes the following big ideas. • "Provides tangible tools for addressing the complex work of reconciling history, race, and justice" (Winn, 2018, p. 36). • Being mindful of the language we use to talk about and to students from different backgrounds than ours is the foundation to healthy relationships (Winn, 2018).	Adopting this stance raises the following questions. • How do you speak about your students? • How do you speak to your students? • How does your school community speak about your students?
Futures Matter	Taking a pedagogical stance that futures matter includes the following big ideas. • "Points to the need to excavate spaces wherein all children are actively encouraged to imagine, and have optimism about, multiple pathways forward" (Winn, 2021, p. 531). • "Serves to generate creativity, imagination, curiosity, and ambitious outlooks regarding black children's future selves and communities" (Winn, 2021, p. 536).	Adopting this stance raises the following questions. • What do you dream teaching and learning will be like fifty years from now? • How would you like your classroom or school to look fifteen years from now?' • What would a liberatory future of schools look, feel, and sound like? For students? For teachers?
Mindset Matters	Taking a pedagogical stance that mindset matters includes the following big idea. • What we say and do comes from our thinking habits. We must continually reflect on our thinking and belief systems because our thoughts matter.	Adopting this stance raises the following questions. • What does your language reveal about your mindset? What do your actions reveal about your mindset? • How do you think about your students from historically marginalized communities?

Figure 5.4: Reflection prompts for Winn's (2018, 2021) restorative justice paradigm.

Accountability, if done with true reconciliation, requires an understanding of greater context. To dive deeper into these pedagogical stances, we must consider how the stances of history and race are present and the implications for justice, language, futures, and mindset. We must reflect and learn through this lens so we can unlearn and be productive agitators. In Winn's (2018, 2021) five pedagogical stances for restorative justice, she discusses how race is informed by history. For example, as you make steps toward accountability that will shift a school's culture, you must unpack the intersection between race and history and the subsequent harm-induced trauma. Let's look at an example. Figure 5.5 shows how Jacobē unpacks the harm she experienced in schools as a student, how that affects her as a teacher, and the implications it raises for her students. In this instance, Jacobē uses two pedagogical stances—history matters and race matters—to put sources of harm in context. This exercise allows her to peel back the layers of both her experiences and those of her students. To complete this exercise for yourself, view the "Unpacking Harm" reproducible (page 140).

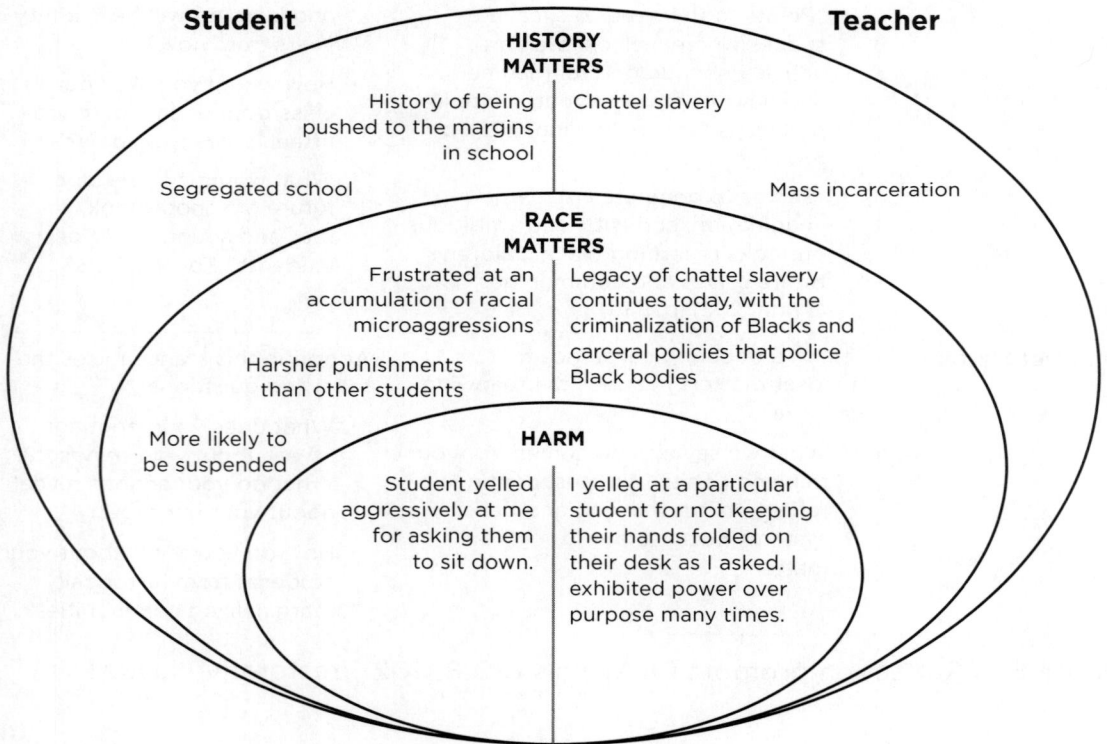

Figure 5.5: An example of unpacking harm.

Jacobē found this activity to be challenging and insightful. She uncovered that she needs to learn a little bit more about the local politics and histories of some of the districts in which she works to better understand the issues they present and how she might advocate for change.

Once we understand more about the context, we must engage in justice and be productive agitators. Winn (2018) explains why understanding our historical context is essential to justice work:

> Justice Matters brings to the forefront social movements that dare to imagine a world where everyone—irrespective of race, ethnicity, socioeconomic status, gender, sexuality, or ability—is able to live with dignity and is recognized as belonging . . . [In education], justice looks like grappling with history and engaging in what needs to be done so that all families and their children receive justice in the form of access to high-quality teaching and learning opportunities. (p. 37)

When justice reflects the practice of freedom and liberation from harm-induced trauma, students are freed from labels and categories that do not reflect their full humanity, as they experience having their identity affirmed, validated, and celebrated. What does it mean to educate students as a practice of freedom? Transformative justice is collective justice and freedom on both sides, for both teachers and students. This means making wrongs right in a way that both educators and students can come to a shared agreement (Winn, 2018). In terms of creating a shift in schooling culture, not only do we need to lean into history, race, futures, and justice mattering, but we must lean into language mattering.

At one of the schools Jacobē worked for previously, Jacobē remembers sitting in the teacher's lounge grading papers and eating lunch. She remembers one of the teachers making jokes about one of their more difficult students. She made derogatory comments about him and his mother. Jacobē remembers internally pausing and staying silent. One of her other colleagues jumped into the conversation a couple of minutes later and stated that they were talking about human beings and someone's child. Jacobē later felt regret for not speaking up. Her colleague was 100 percent right. As educators, we must be mindful of how we use language to speak to and about our students, especially those who come from different communities or have different beliefs or values from our own. Language matters are at the heart of Winn's (2018) work because it provides tangible tools for addressing the complex world of reconciling history, race, and justice.

To Winn's (2018) pedagogical stances we would add the stance of mindsets matter. What we say and do comes out of our beliefs and mindset. Our thinking habits are rooted in our cultural competence, our historical knowledge, and our socialization. To move toward transformative justice we must lean continually into thinking about our thinking. We also must listen with understanding and empathy to a school's community members and consider what they are telling us about their needs. Lastly, we do all of these things because futures matter. To be an authentic educator, we must keep not only an eye on justice now, but an eye on the futures of our students as they must not be stymied by killing their dreams. This means trying our best as teachers to do no harm.

SHIFTING CULTURE AND RELEASING HARM IN PARTNERSHIP

Authentic teachers undertake the responsibility to shift the culture of schooling and classrooms. There is power in self-reflection, but this method alone will not sufficiently promote school improvement. As teachers, we cannot do this alone. We must partner with our students and learn of their harms and needs as well as how they intersect with ours.

One strategy we love to help educators learn about that focuses on the needs and desires of their students is called Empathy 360, so called because it is multi-directional and invites teachers, students, and students' families to participate. We also use it to help educators and students learn more about each other to promote empathy and understanding. It helps both educators and students to see each other as humans. We use Empathy 360 both in our coaching sessions with teachers and in our school change efforts. Empathy dialogues are small-group or one-to-one conversations where participants ask one another open-ended questions to better understand a person's experiences, feelings, emotions, behaviors, and needs. Teachers can use empathy dialogues with students to disrupt the traditional power dynamics of a classroom, which can also serve as a source of harm. Consider the following steps for establishing empathy dialogues within classrooms.

- Identify students as possible participants based on different social, ethnic, and academic groups; engagement; and so on. Ensure you have a range of students.
  - Give students a choice. Do they want to engage with you one-on-one or in a small group with other students?
- Formally invite students who are identified as possible participants to take part in the dialogues (include place, time, length of meeting, and snacks).
  - Ensure meetings are accessible (after school, in class, during lunch, and so on).
- If conversing with a small group, arrange the physical setting in a circle.

- Create agreements on how you'll work together.
    - What are the conditions? Here are some potential ones:
        i. No voice is privileged over another
        ii. One mic: one voice at a time
        iii. Confidentiality
- Share the purpose of the time together.
    - The conversations result in a plan of action for improving the classroom.
- Engage in dialogue where teachers are asking students their opinions and students are asking the teacher their opinion. See figure 5.6 for possible questions to get you started.
- Set up a time for students to ask their families questions or for you to ask the families questions. See figure 5.6 for possible questions to get you started.

Teachers Interview Students	Students Interview Teachers	Teachers Interview Families and Caregivers
• Tell me about a time you enjoyed yourself in school. • What is one word you'd use to describe our class? • Tell me about a time when you were frustrated in class. • What would a joyful classroom look like?	• Tell me about a time you felt good as a teacher. • Tell me about a time you felt bad as a teacher. • What does a joyful classroom look like to you? • If you had three wishes for our class, what would they be?	• What would a joyful and good school look like for your child? Why? • What is one word you'd use to describe your child's learning experience? • What would you like to see more of in your child's schooling? • Is there anything you wish I knew or better understood about your child?

Figure 5.6: Sample prompts to use during an empathy dialogue.

*Visit **go.SolutionTree.com/diversityandequity** for a free reproducible version of this figure.*

After completing the dialogue, allow time for participants to reflect on what they've learned. Figure 5.7 (page 132) offers teachers prompts to journal about their experience and to collect information they learn about their students. After synthesizing what they've learned, teachers may choose to share their insights with students and invite their feedback.

What are students telling you?

What are students feeling?

What are students thinking?

What might students be asking you to do?

Figure 5.7: Journal prompts for teachers.

*Visit **go.SolutionTree.com/diversityandequity** for a free reproducible version of this figure.*

As teachers reflect on what they've learned, they should be careful to not jump to conclusions; it's helpful to suspend judgment and practice being curious. Empathy dialogues are a great starting place to cultivating a justice-oriented classroom.

A second strategy for shifting culture in partnership is a school audit. We encourage schools and educators to engage in an audit of the curriculum and policies in their respective school contexts, considering the implications for their students. They should leverage the previous two tools as a precursor to reflecting on the policies and curricula in their school contexts. Note that audits will occur in several different styles or modalities depending on the designer's preference. Some may decide to collect school documents, interview students, interview teachers, conduct surveys, and so on. Others may choose just a couple of these components. We are providing you with a series of guiding questions to consider as you examine curriculum and policies in schools. Consider the following steps for implementing a curriculum and policy audit.

- Recruit students for the improvement team. Involve them in the creation, outreach, and recruitment of the team. Have a diverse student body represented. Notice whether historically marginalized identities are represented.

- Provide training for students. Co-create the problem that you're looking to solve (if you have one). Co-create a student-friendly research question. Co-create interview and survey questions.

Use the guiding questions in figure 5.8 (page 134) to assist you in the process.

After conducting the audit, students and teachers work together to collect and analyze data using empathy mapping, as demonstrated in figure 5.9 (page 135). If we want to create better futures, then involving our students in the process is important to cultivating human- and student-centered futures. The collaboration and partnership between educators and students to conduct and analyze the data create empathy and understanding.

Curriculum Audit Guiding Questions	Belonging Guiding Questions	Policy Audit Guiding Questions
• Whose voices are centered or prioritized as a part of the learning experience? • Does the curriculum consider varying perspectives on the same topic? Does it account for non-White, non-Eurocentric perspectives on the information? • Are the modalities by which students demonstrate their learning varied and responsive to contemporary cultures? • How frequently do teachers assess students? What is the purpose of these particular assessments? • How are students invited to be collaborators or co-creators of the learning content? • What elements of interdisciplinary learning are afforded to students? How does this advance anti-racist ideology? • Are the needs of neurodiverse and multilingual learners taken into consideration in the curriculum design process? • What is the frequency of traditional, dominant narratives in relation to nuanced and varied experiences? • Is the curriculum designed to center the teacher's knowledge or that of the student?	• How included do you feel in your classroom? • To what extent do you believe your teacher cares about you? • To what extent do you feel like you matter at school? • To what extent do you feel respected in your school? • How much are you encouraged to share your voice in school? • To what extent do you feel your teacher encourages you? • In what ways do the structures of the school day support relationship building? • Does the school have an advisory or some other mechanism to check in on students? • For teachers, to what extent do you feel valued? • For teachers, to what extent do you feel like you belong? • For teachers, to what extent do you feel like your voice is respected and important?	• What are the policies outlining behavioral expectations in your school, and what are the consequences for breaking them? • How do behavioral policies and expectations privilege particular groups of students while marginalizing others? • Conduct a quantitative frequency tally of suspension data. What do you notice? Are there any trends or perspectives that warrant further reflection? • How are students' voices taken into consideration with designing policies or associated practices? • In what ways do the policies currently in existence emphasize White supremacist ideology and beliefs? What would it look like or require for the school or institution to shift away from these ideas? • How are the policies reflective of the beliefs held by the faculty and staff of the institutions? • Are any of the noted or described policies designed to impart long-term trauma on students? • What policies and practices currently exist within the school that center students and see them from a holistic standpoint?

Figure 5.8: Potential audit questions.

*Visit **go.SolutionTree.com/diversityandequity** for a free reproducible version of this figure.*

SAY	DO
Students say . . .	Students do . . .
What quotes and defining words did the student use?	*What actions or behaviors did you notice?*
Educators say . . .	Educators do . . .
What quotes and defining words did the educators use?	*What actions or behaviors did you notice?*
THINK	**FEEL**
Students think . . .	Students feel . . .
What thoughts did the student mention? What does this suggest about their beliefs?	*What emotions did the students report feeling?*
Educators think . . .	Educators feel . . .
What thoughts did the educators mention? What does this suggest about their beliefs?	*What emotions did the educators report feeling?*

Figure 5.9: Empathy Map.

*Visit **go.SolutionTree.com/diversityandequity** for a free reproducible version of this figure.*

After engaging in this empathy mapping activity, consider the following practices for discussing with students what you learned:

- Work together to identify key needs: Avoid deficit perspectives and solutions. Leave conclusions and solutions until the next steps.

- Work together to uncover improvement insights: What insights have you gained about your students' and teachers' experiences and needs? What bright spots emerge? What tensions do you notice? What does this suggest about potential approaches to addressing the problem?

- Work together to determine the next steps.

To shift culture and create new expressions of culture that reject White body supremacy and disrupt trauma caused by harm, we must recognize that history matters, race matters, justice matters, language matters, futures matter, and mindsets matter. If teachers hope to play a role in collective healing, they must be willing to be disruptors: "We need to create the social and cultural disruptions needed to help a culture heal and grow up" (Menakem, 2017, p. 257). Figure 5.10 illustrates how leaning into the transformative justice principles can create social and cultural disruptions, which can in turn lead to healing and a different future.

Figure 5.10: A path to disruptive healing.

Disruptive healing from trauma involves first recognizing and then moving through the pain in ways that choose integrity over fear and standing in that fear with integrity to move toward the unknown (Menakem, 2017). As you embark on your journey of cultivating disruptive healing and disrupting trauma, consider working with a healing professional to support you in the work. In addition to professional support, consider the following practices to engage in the work.

- **Disrupt in community with others:** Who are your people? Find them and work together for change and healing.

- **Work to disrupt with both low-effort, high-impact strategies and high-effort, high-impact strategies:** Low-effort, high-impact strategies or actions require relatively little time, resources, or energy but have a significant positive effect or outcome. In contrast, high-effort, high-impact strategies or actions demand a considerable amount of time, resources, or effort but, in return, have a substantial and meaningful impact. The work can happen in tandem at multiple levels. A school or classroom could have a mix of both strategies. Or one might start with a quick win. A quick win refers to an action or strategy you can implement rapidly, and it may produce immediate positive results or benefits. It's a way to achieve success or demonstrate progress in a short period, often used to build momentum or morale. Quick wins are typically smaller-scale initiatives you can complete swiftly, and they serve as stepping stones toward larger goals. What is a quick win you can do? What areas need more concentrated, collaborative effort?

- **Use antidotes for the problems while you work on the trauma that feels outside of your locus of control:** For example, if you are using a curriculum mandated by your district, how might you center students' identities and joy within it?

- **Resist the urge to respond in ways that create more pain:** Often humans respond to fear and conflict from a place of hurt rather than wholeness. This can create more pain and trauma. Consider when something is bubbling up in your body. Acknowledge it and reflect on it. Use meditations, body scan practices, yoga, therapy, and other techniques to process before responding.

- **Use students, caregivers, and parents as assets in your planning and implementation process:** Utilizing students and parents as assets in the planning and implementation process involves recognizing their strengths, skills, and contributions to enhance the overall educational experience. For example, organize a system where parents can regularly engage you in a feedback loop, or create ways for parents or caregivers to volunteer in the classroom.

Pause and Ponder

Pause and ponder the following questions considering what you've read.

- Do you have a practice for processing school-related trauma? If so, what is your process?
- What might need to shift?
- Who or what might you seek out for support in identifying and addressing the trauma and moving toward liberation?

SUMMING UP

Does this feel like an enormous task? That's OK. You're not alone! Don't allow fear or doubt to sideline you. Start small. Start with what's right in front of you. Start with yourself by noticing where harm, pain, or trauma shows up for you in the classroom. Use the tools you've learned in this chapter as a starting point and get curious about where that might lead you.

Consider the following key takeaways from this chapter.

- Harm lives in all of us and manifests through behaviors, speech, and actions.

- Within schooling contexts, harm can exist at numerous intersections.

- We must unpack the way schooling may have harmed us to be truly disruptive and anti-racist in our approach.

- Race, history, language, justice, and mindset matters are crucial to understanding the context of a school's culture. Culture is inclusive of the harm that exists or has been enacted.

- Addressing harm can lead to disruptive healing.

Processing Harm and Moving Forward

Take a moment to reflect on a time a student experienced harm in your classroom. Choose one of the following practices to reflect on the experience and process any feelings that arise.

Practice 1: Writing an apology to students

- Acknowledge what you did wrong.

- Write a genuine apology explaining why you are sorry.

- Let the student know what action you will take to repair the harm.

Practice 2: Write a letter to your early self

- Start your letter off by showing care for your early self.

- What is something positive you'd have benefitted from hearing back then?

- Based on your teaching experiences, what would you go back and tell your early self?

- What advice would you give your early self?

Now that you've completed the practice, take a moment to reflect. What feelings came up during and after the exercise? Do you feel energized, drained, relieved, sad, or something else? Whatever your experience, offer yourself compassion. To close out this practice, move your body. Run, walk, or dance to release any pent-up emotions that come to the surface. This discharge is helpful for both your emotional and your physical well-being (Menakem, 2017).

Reference

Menakem, R. (2017). My grandmother's hands: Racialized trauma and the pathway to mending our hearts and bodies. *Las Vegas, NV: Central Recovery Press.*

Unpacking Harm

Pull back the layers of both students and educators. To do this, begin with the student side of the graphic organizer in the "harm" circle. What is the harm you've caused students? Fill it in. Then, reflect on the part race plays in the harm you've caused. Then, consider what the history is in the local context that impacts this harm as well. Then, repeat the same process for the teacher side of the circle.

HISTORY MATTERS
Historically, what have been the dynamics in your local context?

RACE MATTERS
How might bias impact the experience? What is the role of race in this situation?

HARM
What is the haarm you've caused? Or experienced?

After completing the activity, take a moment to reflect on the following questions.

- *What did this activity uncover for you?*

- *What might you need to learn?*

- *What might you need to unlearn?*

- *How can you center justice and student futures in this work?*

CHAPTER 6

DREAMS OF AN AUTHENTIC FUTURE

In a collaborative team session, Jacobē led the session participants in dreaming about what they desire for their great, great, great grandchildren's education. Many participants named they want schools to hold space for students to be curious, to have their inner spirits flourish, and to be allowed to be fully human. One of the unintended consequences of this activity was that one teacher built upon it to get her students to dream and create using an Afrofuturism lens. The teacher asked students, "How does freedom dreaming lend itself to alternative futures?" Then, she replicated the dreaming activity she'd completed with Jacobē. Students crafted their own futuristic vision through whatever creative medium they wished to express that vision.

As teachers divest from the status quo and address harm in their classroom and school contexts, they inevitably reach a point of no return. They can't go back to the way things were, but what are they moving toward? It's a question of "So now what?" If you've ever experienced this place in your professional or personal life, you know the feeling. It's a pause, an empty space. It's a time of uncertainty. How can teachers navigate the experience and find their way forward? In chapter 5 (page 111), we discussed how addressing harm can lead to disruptive healing. In this chapter, we see our imagination as a path toward a different future. Do you ever get stuck when trying to imagine something new or different? When Jacobē gets stuck, she turns to Afrofuturism for inspiration and as a cultural lens to see and imagine beyond what's in front of us.

This lens comprises the following themes.

- **Afrofuturism:** A Black cultural lens used to consider the future.
- **Deliberate dreaming:** Daring to dream and imagine limitless possibilities.
- **Centering humanity:** Seeing the whole person when engaging as opposed to what they represent to you.

141

- **Habits of being, living, and teaching:** Choosing to show up in a manner that incorporates these elements, discussed in more detail throughout this chapter.

Because liminal experiences tend to be abstract, we draw on the cultural aesthetic of Afrofuturism to make this chapter's themes more concrete and tangible. In this chapter, we explore how centering humanity and deliberate dreaming allow teachers to manifest new habits of being, living, and teaching to chart their path through the unknown toward greater equity for all.

Guiding Questions

In this chapter, we focus on the following questions:

- Why do we need disruption to build a new educational world?
- How would we step into this world that doesn't yet exist?
- What thinking habits do we need to have?
- What does it mean to freedom dream?
- What does it mean to dream about a new world?
- How do we create space for our students to dream?
- How do we invite our students into the process so that we're collectively creating this new world together?

INTRODUCING AFROFUTURISM

Throughout this book, we've explored the many reasons the institution of schooling must change. In some ways committing to making the change is the easy part. Once we've done that, we must consider the question, What *can* it become?

In "A Few Rules for Predicting the Future," Octavia E. Butler (2000) writes, "There's no single answer that will solve all of our future problems. There's no magic bullet. Instead, there are thousands of answers—at least. You can be one of them if you choose to be" (p. 165). This is the privilege and responsibility that every teacher disrupting status quo education carries. We step into the unknown and take up the responsibility to create something new.

Afrofuturism offers us a wealth of tools for this task. It seeks to change and explore critical narratives of different worlds that draw on the past, technology, Black culture, and the imagination. Essentially, it allows us to imagine what could exist if we weren't confined by existing structures.

What exactly is Afrofuturism? Because Black people in North America have had to navigate "having the full human experience," Afrofuturism seeks to "create in ways that value humanity" (Womack, 2013, p. 9). To do this Ytasha L. Womack (2013) locates Afrofuturism at "an intersection of imagination, technology, the future, and liberation" (p. 9). It centers on imagining and dreaming possible futures through a Black cultural lens. We believe that humanization, as contextualized in this chapter, cultivates spaces of authenticity for educators. The Afrofuture Strategies Institute (n.d.) offers this definition of Afrofuturism:

> An intersectional, multitemporal, multidimensional, and interdisciplinary approach to the future. Also called a liberation movement, Afrofuturism empowers [Black bodies] to craft destinies and realities of inclusion, health, joy, and prosperity using speculative modalities such as science fiction, surrealism, magical realism, and horror. The cultural movement investigates the intersection of race, technology, and science while being inspired by mythologies, legends, spiritual practices, and cosmologies from Africa and the diaspora. Afrofuturism serves as a vehicle to liberate Black bodies and all humans.

Thus, Afrofuturism explores various alternative futures for Black people that are not necessarily a utopia but an alternative possibility of reality (Steinskog, 2018). As a vehicle to liberation, Afrofuturism can be a type of healing that is located in Black liberation movements and the arts. Examples of Afrofuturism in today's society are the movie *Black Panther* (Coogler, 2018), *Kindred* (Butler, 1979) and Octavia Butler's other books, the album *Black Is King* by Beyoncé (2020), and *Dirty Computer* (Monáe, 2018).

Let's look at one example to illustrate how these tenets are manifest. In *Black Panther*, director Ryan Coogler (2018) uses Afrofuturism to disrupt the status quo narratives about Afro people. In the film, Coogler uses technology to imagine an avant-garde society rooted in Afro-cultural ways of being and doing—a society where the Wakandan people were never subject to racism or White supremacy, a society that centers the liberation and freedom of Afro people. This daring vision of alternative futures offers a message of hope and empowerment.

Just like *Black Panther* disrupts the status quo in terms of narratives surrounding people, culture, and society—and created healing for so many Black kids—teachers disrupting education's status quo can dream of practices where all students see themselves in teaching and learning. Afrofuturism offers educators:

- A lens for dreaming to disrupt the racist, classist status quo in education and enter into a state of emerging as an authentic educator who looks beyond today and is part of change work

- Tools and technologies to disrupt oppression and racism in teaching and learning

- Courage to dream of a different future where all can learn in ways that validate and affirm who they are

Saidiya Hartman (2019), an acclaimed writer, explains that "Black feminism is the desire for the end of the world as we know it" (p. 366). That is what we want to do as authentic educators. Transformation starts with us. We need to shift how we see and feel about each other. brown (2017) says, "If we begin to understand ourselves as a practice ground for transformation, we can transform the world" (p. 87). By beginning to transform ourselves, we can begin to transform both teaching and learning.

CENTERING HUMANITY AS A LENS FOR DREAMING

The banking model of education often used today treats students as objects and utilizes a skill, drill, and memorization approach to learning that encourages students to receive the information and store it (Freire, 1968/2000). Thus it promotes passivity and a killing of curiosity. In today's society:

> The top-down, teach-and-test method, in which learning is motivated by a system of rewards and punishments rather than by curiosity or by any real, felt desire to know, is well designed for indoctrination and obedience training but not much else. (p. Gray, 2013)

These reasons, as well as ones mentioned in previous chapters, point to the dehumanizing practices occurring in schools as they cause students to devalue a part of themselves. Moments of empathy and kindness *do* exist; we have seen them. But under the current system, schools sometimes unwittingly impede a student's humanity as a result of being beholden to external demands. Students are often seen as test scores, reading levels, or learning classifications rather than as the beautifully complex and autonomous humans they actually are.

Teachers committed to equity for all must dream of the possibilities and alternative futures for schools—futures where students' and teachers' full humanity can flourish. You may be wondering, what does it mean to center humanity? Drawing on the work of Freire (1968/2000) and others, M del Carmen Salazar (2013) found five key ideas that are necessary to pursue humanizing pedagogy and pursue one's own humanity.

1. **Developing the full person is important for humanization:** For example, we must see students beyond their cognitive beings as people who are also both social and emotional beings.

2. **To deny someone else's humanization is also to deny one's own (Freire, 1968/2000):** Dehumanizing practices impact not only those humans who have been oppressed but also those who have done the oppressing.

3. **The journey for humanization is an individual and collective endeavor (Salazar, 2013):** It involves both students and teachers working together to engage in mutual humanization through the development of critical consciousness. It requires an increased consciousness of one's own contribution to reproducing oppressive structures.

4. **Critical reflection and action are necessary to transform the world and the structures "that impede our own and others' humanness, thus facilitating liberation for all" (Salazar, 2013, p. 128):** For example, lessons that relate to the real world and social justice can be used to develop critical reflection on issues related to race, class, power, ability, gender, and so on.

5. **"Educators are responsible for promoting a more fully human world through their pedagogical principles and practices" (Salazar, 2013, p. 128):** This means the practices of educators should reflect the belief that students are fully human. For example, educators should consider the socioeconomic and sociocultural resources that are relevant to students' lives, the type of relationships they are building with students, and how a student's culture is positioned as mattering and as an asset.

One of Jacobē's former teachers required her college class to write weekly responses to the class readings in the form of more formal writings. Each response needed to be a specific format, length, font, and so on. Jacobē dreaded writing these responses every week. For her, it took the joy out of the readings. Partway through the semester, Jacobē asked if she could respond in various other formats for the weekly assignment. The answer was no. Juxtapose this to another course Jacobē was taking simultaneously where there also were weekly responses, yet they could be in any format as long as they met the common criteria. For Jacobē the freedom to express herself through podcasts, interviews, writing, or other creative measures brought the class readings to life. It was invigorating. Where one class allowed Jacobē the freedom and flexibility to flourish, the other was stifling. In the first classroom, Jacobē's full humanity wasn't able to flourish because only one way of knowing was championed as being able to demonstrate critical thinking—while in the second classroom, which had the same expectations for critical thinking, Jacobē's ways of being and knowing were accepted and celebrated in the demonstration of the learnings.

As educators, we are responsible for creating learning experiences that honor students' unique ways of knowing and creating as assets. By beginning to transform ourselves and how we move in the world, we can begin to create a more human world.

Afrofuturism offers tools for dreaming of a new way of approaching education—one that sees students' unique qualities as assets and affirms their humanity.

CENTERING HUMANITY, AFROFUTURISM, AND TEACHING

In the history of North America, minoritized people have had to negotiate their humanity in order to live a fully human experience in society (Womack, 2013). Just as Afrofuturism strives to value humanity, teachers must also strive to create educational environments that honor students' full expression of their humanity. Let's return to Afrofuturism to help us consider the following questions about our teaching practice.

- What would education look like if it had never been touched by colonization?
- How are we teaching in ways that promote and embrace students as fully human?
- How might we use technology to inspire and imagine a different future?
- Are the spiritual mythologies of the diaspora present or included in teaching and learning?
- How are folks on the margins of society oppressed?
- How are we engaging in critical reflection?
- How can we imagine teaching and learning that provides space for students to be creative, critical thinkers?

Cultivating a practice of reflecting on such questions gives us the tools to disrupt oppressive practices and create the new world we dream of. Afrofuturism has no boundaries of time, race, and space. It has no creative limits. Afrofuturism can bring that awareness of what world building looks like. It offers us the tools we need to create a new world rather than replicating the old.

Pause to Reflect

Let's engage in some creative world building. Write, draw, or discuss with others:

- How do you imagine a school where all are recognized and operationalized as fully human?
- How do you see yourself as a change agent in this imagined school?
- How does this imagined school look? Feel? Sound?

To be the change, and for change to begin in us, we must take creative license to dream. Toni Morrison didn't see herself in any stories she read (CultureContent, 2012). She had to dream up and create the stories she wanted to read. Morrison (2008) in *A Mercy* says, "I dream a dream that dreams back at me" (p. 137). We also must dare to dream and create the school and teaching practices in service of freedom.

DARING TO DREAM

The following is a conversation between Reshma and her eldest daughter, Deepika (not her real name). Reshma was curious to know how her daughter saw her school and what it would look like if she could dream of another learning experience.

> *Reshma: What do you dream about?*
>
> *Deepika: Sometimes I dream about crazy things, like cats.*
>
> *Reshma: Do you like cats?*
>
> *Deepika: I love cats.*
>
> *Reshma: What do you dream about when it comes to school?*
>
> *Deepika: When I'm daydreaming about school, sometimes I think about taking field trips to a water park or something like that.*
>
> *Reshma: OK, what do you wish you could have in school?*
>
> *Deepika: I sometimes wish I could do anything. Like, it could be a cooking school. A cooking school in school [would be great] because it would be a humongous school. We could have a doctor's university. There would be three huge rooms, and one would be a teacher's university and the other ones would just be, like, subjects that you have to learn.* [Author's note: Deepika wants to be a teacher when she grows up.]
>
> *Reshma: But what would the students be doing?*
>
> *Deepika: They would be doing all the things that I just said.* [At this point, she rolls her eyes at Reshma.]

Following the conversation with her daughter, Reshma also asked teachers the following question: "What do you dream about as an educator?" The responses varied, but included:

- Winning the lottery (who doesn't?!)
- Having more time off

- Having the ability to teach how they want to teach
- Having more money for books and other resources

When probed a bit more, their responses were a bit stunted. Teachers couldn't fully articulate what they wanted to do differently but could identify immediate experiences that were hindering the type of classroom they had hoped to cultivate at the outset of their career. For example, at one school, teachers bemoaned the use of copious data trackers that required additional paperwork that they spent their prep periods completing.

Reshma was interested to see the difference in perspective between Deepika and the adult teachers. Some might explain the difference in perspective by pointing to age or financial obligations (hello, student loans!). They're not wrong. But notice Deepika's joy. Her confidence. The adults didn't seem to share that enthusiasm, that boundless optimism, that belief in possibility. The diminished emotions are grounded in a lack of autonomy. Children are free to dream in a way that most adults lose. Dreaming as adults often means conforming to societal expectations—many of which are grounded in White supremacy (chapter 2, page 25).

Pause and Ponder

Pause and ponder the following questions considering what you've read.

- When was the last time you dared to dream about your life as an educator?
- When was the last time you encouraged your students to dream of a different experience than the one they have in front of them?
- What is within your locus of control to dream about?

If asked to identify a specific moment or instance in which they stopped dreaming, teachers couldn't name the exact details (for example, date, time, place, and so on). However, they could point to a particular feeling they had. The word cloud in figure 6.1 represents some of the common phrases they expressed when thinking about when their mindset around teaching began to shift.

job   room

control   **exhausted**

ownership   expectations

critical   innovation

just   **demoralized**

tired   creativity

defeated   fun

bored

routine

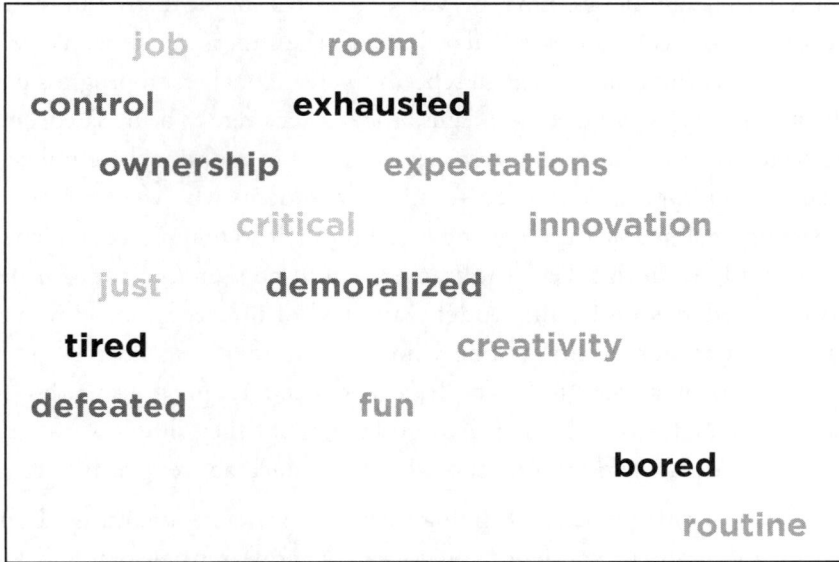

Figure 6.1: A word cloud exploring teachers' mindsets around teaching.

This word cloud illustrates the tensions that teachers navigate as their dreams about teaching fade. They also shared the following circumstances that influenced the emotions that shifted their perspective on teaching.

- Evaluations by individuals who often projected their personal and subjective perspectives on the teacher as opposed to their practice

- Overemphasis on testing or data associated with tests

- Not having the autonomy to adjust curricula to represent their students or engage in other substantive learning experiences

- Colleagues who consciously or unconsciously marginalized their capacities as a teacher

These circumstances are representative of larger systemic problems around schooling. Schools represent a hierarchical process in which much of a teacher's autonomy is restricted due to factors that are outside of their control. As we explored in chapter 3 (page 55), systems do what they are designed to do—especially those that do not humanize the individual. Traditional schooling does not encourage teachers or students to dream of an equitable world or provide them the tools to create it, stripping away all elements of authenticity in the process.

In our current schooling system, standards take precedence over students. This results in a reductionist approach to teaching, learning, and allowing school to be a space for joy. For example, Reshma was working with a sizable district in the Bronx. She had three schools in this particular district. The superintendent, likely under pressure from the chancellor, asked all schools to create trackers to progress monitor the students' mastery of particular standards. The trackers were to be updated a number of times each week. School administrators were asked to monitor these trackers and had an additional layering of trackers to monitor students who were deemed pushable to passing or slippable from passing based on their state test scores. Depending on who might have been asked, the trackers could be seen as a tool for helping teachers and leaders identify the students in need of intervention. However, the reality is that an accountability tool only further dehumanizes students—reducing them to numbers on a page (for example, attendance rate, previous grades, scores, and socioeconomic factors). Standards are valuable, but they should serve students and teachers; academic performance should not be valued above their full humanity.

In the midst of current schooling practices and policies, dreaming about and manifesting a liberatory experience can be seen as nonessential. After all, dreaming requires us to imagine a future or experience that bucks current expectations. AnnMarie Baines, Diana Medina, and Caitlin Healy (2023) note:

> Schools are designed to reinforce expectations of conformity where young people who do not fit dominant expectations are policed, labeled "at risk," pushed to the margins, ranked as less competent, and seen as less successful (Baines, 2014). These expectations, defined by White-supremacy culture, have characteristics such as the worship of the written word and the assertion that there is only one right way to do something. (p. 6)

Throughout this book we have discussed the implicit and explicit ways in which we have been socialized to internalize beliefs of a system as it exists in schools and institutions. The oppressive tendencies of a school's structure can result in the eradication of play, dreaming, and liberation. The methods in which White supremacy exists are not as blatant as extremists usurping school boards. Rather, they are as innocent as curricular choices, class programming, grading, and discipline. These factors are reflective of a mold that schools seek to imprint on students—mandating who they should be, how they should grow up, the methods of speaking they should use, and so on. All of this is in opposition to the idea of manifesting an identity of their choosing.

When thinking about the ways in which we might reimagine or dream of school, we encourage educators to consider the domains in which liberatory dreaming can take root: structure, curriculum, and student agency. Table 6.1 breaks down what this could look like as well as the questions we might pose.

Table 6.1: Rethinking the Elements of Schooling From a
Liberatory Lens

Element	Description	Guiding Questions	Examples of Dreaming in Action
Structure	This is essentially the nuts and bolts of how a school operates. It includes but is not limited to: • Schedule • Class programming • Explicit operating values, mission, and policies • Implicit policies • Disciplinary codes • Beliefs around the purpose of schooling and what this means for student performance • Grading policies and expectations	• What is the purpose of existing structures, schedules, classes, and so on? • Do the existing structures meet the needs of all students? • How do the existing structures support humanizing pedagogies or experiences for students? • What is the ideal life experience for students postschool? • When students leave this space after ____ years, how will they reflect on the experience? • How would students describe the ultimate purpose for attending this school?	In two schools we recently visited, there were examples of students choosing the classes they take versus having a teacher determine this information. For example, students can self-select into an AP class as opposed to being "chosen" by a teacher for this experience. If students do not feel as though the class is a good fit, regardless of the point in the school year, they can swap into another section. For example, a Regents-track student can opt into an AP course without teacher "approval." In addition to being able to choose their academic track, students are able to collaborate with teachers to create a course of their own choosing. For example, one school has a literature and cinema course that students can take in lieu of or in addition to AP courses.

continued →

Element	Description	Guiding Questions	Examples of Dreaming in Action
Curriculum	Curriculum is thought of as content that is taught. However, curriculum refers not just to explicit content, but also to implicit ideas that reinforce societal beliefs or expectations. Curriculum can include: • Expectations that reinforce teacher-pleasing behaviors • Cultural cues that are seen as normative • Social ideas that are prevalent within the micro and macro community • Ideas that reinforce Whiteness or White supremacist behaviors • Marginalization of noncentered voices or emphasis on White voices as a source of knowledge	• How does the information that students learn help to disrupt problematic practices in society? How does the content reinforce this information? • What role or voice do students have in determining the trajectory of the curriculum? • What is the purpose of the curriculum that is being taught? • How does the curriculum reflect needs or concerns from the community? • Are nondominant voices centered in the curriculum design? • What percentage of learning or curricular content is devoted to marginalized voices? How does this compare to the White, heteronormative voices? • Is the curriculum challenging the status quo or reinforcing it?	We have worked with students and teachers to help design the scope and sequence for a course. This process consisted of conducting empathy interviews, auditing existing curricula, and contextualizing the curricular needs within the community. We consider: How would this curriculum reflect the values or beliefs of the community? In a small school we worked with, teachers often felt as though their curriculum was not landing in the way they hoped. Students appeared to be bored with or disengaged in the content. We guided teachers to conduct empathy interviews and create a revised unit of study. Students were asked to authorize the curriculum before execution. In one such instance, students asked for more field trips because they hadn't had the chance to experience them since elementary school.

Element	Description	Guiding Questions	Examples of Dreaming in Action
Student Agency	Educators reflect on how much autonomy students hold within the schooling context. Student agency should consider: • Socioemotional needs of the learner • Physical or spatial request • Contribution to or collaboration on school policies or priorities • Contribution to or collaboration on instructional content	• What is the percentage of student voice or agency within a school? • How is student participation encouraged outside of traditional media such as student government? • How are students encouraged or invited to participate in collaborative experiences with other educators in the building? • What are students' needs? How are students invited to share pressing needs or concerns? • How are students' needs or concerns taken into consideration?	We have seen schools attempted to center students, but such initiatives are still constrained by adult mindsets or perceptions around students' roles. True student agency would potentially mimic a sociocratic approach to decisions. The following paradigms would exist to enable students as true collaborators in learning. • A student advisory council supports the school leadership team. • School scheduling allocates time for students to intentionally be a part of all instructional planning meetings. • Opportunities exist for students to provide unsolicited feedback. • Students can give feedback on policies or pilot alternate solutions. • Students design learning spaces to represent their interests and socioemotional or physical needs.

DREAMING AND DISRUPTION IN A FUTURISTIC WORLD

In a 2020 article for *Vogue*, activist and filmmaker Tourmaline shared what it means or looks like to freedom dream. She said, "Freedom dreams are born when we face harsh conditions not with despair, but with the deep knowledge that these conditions will change—that a world filled with softness and beauty and care is not only possible, but inevitable" (Tourmaline, 2020). As she recommends in her article, and as we have done throughout the course of this book, we begin by asking questions. However, we don't want to ask random questions about freedom dreaming. The questions we pose to you fall within the umbrella of:

- What does it mean to be if we exist in a disrupted world?
- What does it mean to live if we exist in a disrupted world?
- What does it mean to teach and learn if we exist in a disruptive world?

Figure 6.2 illustrates how habits of being, living, and teaching can offer a pathway for disrupting oppressive schooling systems and allowing for dreams.

Dreaming for a Liberated Future

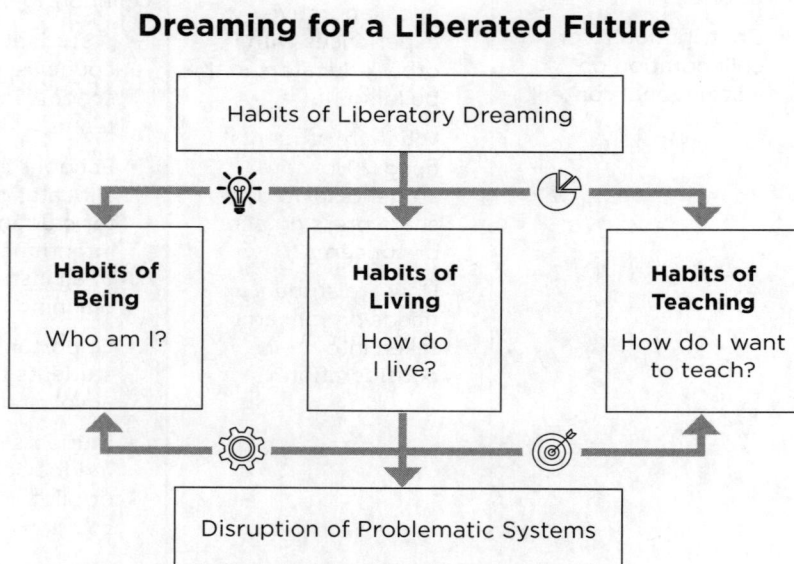

Figure 6.2: A graphic showing the relationship between freedom dreaming, Afrofuturism, and habits for disruption.

To engage in habits of liberatory dreaming you must consider who you are, how you live, and how you desire to teach as a way to disrupt problematic systems. We will dive deeper into each of these components in the next section.

We have continuously encouraged you to reflect on your lived experiences and their impact on your sense of self as well as your practices as a teacher. What would these reflections look like if you could dream of an alternate sense of being, living, or teaching? How are they interconnected? We are not asking you to forget about your lived experiences. Rather, this section is prompting you to dream about what could be if you did not have to conform to large systemic oppressions. In this section, we will explore a series of self-reflective questions for these ideas as well as exploratory concepts based on freedom dreaming.

Habits of Being

The premise of being stems back to early philosophical ideas rooted in non-Western beliefs. We are all familiar with René Descartes's "I think, therefore I am." Preceding this European take on being are ancient Asian texts such as the Bhagavad Gita or Vedas, which explore the ways in which our soul lives within our body. Our soul is confined by the physical body and social structures that impact actions associated with action. We posit that being is essentially who we are, our soul—that is, who we would be if we were not forced to conform or construct to meet the demands and expectations of systemic oppression. The idea of being in a disrupted world means we can choose to show up in a manner that does not prompt judgment or ridicule. The uniqueness of our personalities should be celebrated and encouraged. We should be seen as a whole.

The notion of being includes but is not limited to expressions of self, non-Western modes of thinking, troubling White supremacy, and knowing one's happiness. Table 6.2 invites you to explore habits of being using a series of reflection questions and examples.

Table 6.2: Habits of Being Overview

Habits of Being	Reflection Questions	Definition and Example
Expressions of Self	• Who are you? • How do you want to be seen? • What makes you a whole person? • At your most unfiltered self, who are you? • What brings you joy? • What do you seek from this life?	The ability to speak one's native language or cadence is a form of unrestricted expression of self. One might dream of not having to switch between worlds and inflections because one context might not understand the dialect.
Modes of Thinking	• What patterns are most often associated with your thinking process? • How do you best learn and process information? • What other modes of learning or processing information are best for your personality? • How do you respond to thinking patterns that are different from yours?	Many non-White cultures utilize an oratory method for sharing information or disseminating discourse across a community. This results in people who are more auditory in their process and do not only value the written word.

continued →

Habits of Being	Reflection Questions	Definition and Example
White Supremacy and You	• What elements of White supremacist culture exist within your operating practices? • Which elements of White supremacist culture do you want to remove from your personality? • Which elements of White supremacist culture might you be inclined to keep? How do you ensure these attributes don't oppress others?	White supremacy has several attributes. A few examples are urgency, individualism, prioritizing the written word, and either/or thinking. As American culture is steeped in these values, we have to consider what we would be like if we leaned into community or our personal networks. How would our lives become more enriched?
Your Happiness	• How do you define the idea of happiness? • What is often correlated with your personal happiness? • Are there traces of White supremacy in the things, experiences, and moments of happiness? • How is happiness connected to your modes of thinking?	At the onset of this section, teachers jokingly shared the things that would make them happy if they could dream. The reality is, humans are happiest when they have control over their contexts. Happiness manifests when we know what we are hoping to gain, as an experience, and the non-negotiables we hold in order to obtain it.

Pause and notice your response to what you've read in this table. How do you feel in your body? Relieved? Hopeful? Free? Unsafe? Threatened? Uncertain? Skeptical? How each person responds depends on where they are on the journey to embracing and expressing their authentic self. Regardless of where you might be, we encourage you to continue practicing self-reflection. Understanding who you are without the pressures of society requires a great deal of work. It is important to sit with the questions and process the information accordingly.

Habits of Living

"Can I live?" When the phrase is uttered by folks of color, especially Black people, it is done with an exasperated tone and meant to ask if the person can be allowed to do life on their own terms. When we think about the habits of living in a disrupted, futuristic society, there is a clear correlation to the habits of being that we might adopt. Habits of living refer to the ways in which we are intentionally bucking behaviors or practices that have been modeled by oppressive expectations and structures. Living on our own terms asks us to consider the following questions.

- What life would you live if your soul could be free?

- How would you ensure that joy remained a central point in your life?

- How do you move against oppressive molds that shaped your identity?

Table 6.3 invites you to explore habits of living using a series of reflection questions and examples.

Table 6.3: Habits of Living Overview

Habits of Living	Reflection Questions	Definition and Example
Defining Purpose	• What is your purpose? • What drives your goals and ambitions? • How is your purpose connected to your upbringing? • What purpose in your life would feel liberatory or freeing? • How is your purpose different from your occupation?	For many educators, their purpose might be intricately wrapped up in their career. However, purpose can look distinctly different if we choose to separate the two. One's purpose in life is to live in a manner that prioritizes joy, rest, and connection with other people.
Behaviors, Emotions, and Thoughts	• How are your behaviors, emotions, and thoughts related to the way in which you live? • How are your behaviors, emotions, and thoughts representative of your purpose? • How do your behaviors, emotions, and thoughts liberate your thinking? How might they be representative of oppressive ideas? • How do your behaviors, emotions, and thoughts mirror oppressive behaviors in society? How do they disrupt oppressive behaviors?	Shifting away from a sense of urgency to all activities and dismantling the need for time frames or stamps is one method for cultivating a free life. Many students leave school with the belief that they are only as important as their accomplishments. This impacts associated behaviors, emotions, and thoughts. Urgency and time frames are often tangible outputs of behaviors, emotions, and thoughts that are constrained by oppressive factors.
Establishing an Identity	• Who are you? • Who are you in the absence of all of the extras, accomplishments, or merits you have obtained in your life to date? • What are the ways in which your life has been molded by White supremacy? How can you shuck the yoke of its expectations? • How do you want to be seen? • How can you allow your self-perception to create a space of joy?	Much of who we are is often defined by the contexts we have encountered (for example, socialization). Establishing an identity outside of these contexts requires us to think about how we want to be seen and the attributes associated with this perception.

As with the habits of being, leaning into the habits of living requires one to be intentional and conscientious about all of the decisions that are being made. This can be hard! After all, we sometimes make between 33,000 and 35,000 decisions each day (Reill, 2023). Mindfulness around each can become overwhelming. We recommend that you start by simply naming one aspect from Table 6.3 (page 157) that you want to attend to. Do you want to rethink your purpose? Monitor your behaviors? Once you have picked one bite-sized element, commit to working on it for a time frame that feels manageable for you. You will find that daily attention to this element will manifest in freedom-dreaming-based shifts. It won't be easy given that our society is designed to reward conformity and compliance. Nor are we going to lean into toxic positivity and assume everything will work out. What we can say is that you are worthy of living a life that you dream of—one that is fulfilling, liberating, and authentic to your personality. The implications of this will be profound, not just for you but for your students.

Habits of Teaching and Learning

When we set out to compose this book, we wanted to provide educators with a platform for exploring what it means to be authentic and intentionally humanizing in their pedagogy. There is a connection between authenticity and centering humanity. When one feels like a whole person and leans into their humanity, the veneer of long-standing, societally enforced oppression falls away, thereby allowing for the exploration of what it means to be authentic. Freedom dreaming offers a means for recentering humanity and envisioning a future where you can embody your authentic self in all of life—including in the classroom. Although this begins as inner work, it also extends outward; it becomes manifest as we replace old habits with new ones rooted in our authenticity.

Table 6.4 overviews three habits of teaching and learning in a freedom-based future: (1) alternate sources of knowledge and information, (2) sociocratic approaches to learning, and (3) deconstructed instruction and assessment. Table 6.4 outlines each with reflection questions and examples.

Table 6.4: Habits of Teaching and Learning Overview

Habits of Teaching and Learning	Reflection Questions	Definition and Example
Alternate Sources of Knowledge and Information	• Where do we source knowledge from? • Who is seen as a valid source of knowledge? Are students allowed to contribute, and are they seen as legitimate sources of knowledge? • Whose voice or perspective is centered as being a primary source of knowledge? • What forms of information do you provide to students as they attempt to build their own knowledge? • How are community members seen as legitimate sources of knowledge? • Does the knowledge that is explored in class and school resonate with lived experiences outside of the building?	When having students complete a research project, it would be beneficial if they started by interviewing members of their community. They could use this information as a part of their research process and learn how to hone investigative skills. This legitimizes knowledge that comes from their community as well as their process for finding nontraditional modes of information.
Sociocratic Approaches to Learning	• Who tends to make the decisions in your learning contexts? Within your schools? • What is the percentage of adults making decisions? • What is the percentage of students making decisions? • How are policies reflective of student interest and voices? • Do the policies humanize all bodies within the building?	Sociocratic approaches differ from democratic approaches in that there is more of a ground-up or communal process for gaining consensus on decisions. This can often be time-consuming. However, if the school embeds the time in their schedule and structure for conversations to be had around important decisions and daily needs, then time does not become a hindrance. An example of sociocratic approaches might involve deciding on the school's uniforms policy. Having the students lead the conversation would be one way to place ownership into the hands of students in this case.

continued →

Habits of Teaching and Learning	Reflection Questions	Definition and Example
Deconstructed Instruction and Assessment	• What is the traditional mode of teaching and learning as it occurs in your schooling context? • How often are students centered in their ability to contribute to the conversation? • What assessments are prevalent among others? What is the percentage of these assessments? • How do assessments reflect the interests and readiness of both teachers and learners? • Is the grading system equitable and flexible?	This concept refers to rethinking the ways in which instruction and assessment have been historically done within American schools. There is a very linear process by which students are learning information. They learn information, and then they complete an assessment that is meant to measure their learning. Deconstruction refers to unpacking and probing what counts as knowledge and information. Instruction on a daily basis can vary and does not need to follow the same rote process. This connects to the passions of the teacher as well as passions of the students. The subsequent assessments can also vary in their structure. This also means that the grading policies will be reflective of how students and teachers feel they should be assessed.

These three habits of teaching and learning in a freedom-based future are great ways to begin to dream and implement more human-centered learning practices. Together, these approaches create a more personalized, inclusive, and dynamic educational experience that values and nurtures the whole person. This human-centered focus prepares students not just academically but also emotionally and socially, equipping them with the skills and mindsets needed to thrive in a complex, interconnected world.

Pause and Ponder

Pause and ponder the following questions considering what you've read.

• What elements of Afrofuturism resonate with your personal journey, and how might incorporating these themes into self-reflection enhance your understanding of identity and potential?

• How does Afrofuturism address the intersectionality of race, culture, and identity, and how might engaging with these themes prompt a more nuanced self-reflection?

• How can engaging with Afrofuturist narratives prompt us to reconsider our understanding of resilience, resistance, and empowerment in our personal narratives of self-reflection?

SUMMING UP

Human potential to create new spaces and experiences is unlimited. But to achieve that potential, we must return to the act of dreaming. Rather than diminishing our capacity or contribution to the world, dreaming offers an opportunity for us to think beyond this realm and explore options that are not yet manifest. In order to do so, we have to release the socially constructed inhibitions that impede our desire to break tradition. Find the person you were when you once dreamed on a regular basis. Bring that person back and use their brilliance to imagine and create an innovative future.

Consider the following key takeaways from this chapter.

- Afrofuturism is a complex concept that empowers Black people or those who identify as being a part of the African diaspora to imagine a future that is free of colonialism, White supremacy, and racism. It is the reality of what should have been.

- Leaning on Afrofuturism allows us to imagine a future beyond what currently exists. We can stretch our imaginations and play in ways we could not if were we otherwise confined.

- Disrupting schools through an Afrofuturism lens requires us to freedom dream about what can be done with schools.

- Dreaming requires us to challenge our habits of being and living. This will result in a shift in how we envision teaching and learning practices.

Dreaming Using Afrofuturism

Given what you've read in chapter 6, practice dreaming for yourself and your students. Use the following prompts as your guide.

What are your dreams for your classroom?

What do these dreams look like, sound like, and feel like?

What habits of being would you need to embrace to embody this dream?

Now let's push these boundaries. Choosing one of the elements of Afrofuturism (imagination, technology, the future, liberation, or speculative fiction) draw inspiration to consider:

- A character

- A plot

- A setting

- A theme

- An image

- A technological advancement

Then create a story that puts at least two of these elements in conversation with one another.

Lastly, consider the inspiration your story may bring for the dream classroom you want to cultivate.

EPILOGUE

Thank you for undertaking this journey. We hope that your encounter with each chapter has prompted deep reflection and cultivated immense hope for your practice as an educator. We know none of us is perfect. We are human, imperfect souls. We will at times stray or be socialized away from authenticity. Authenticity is not a static destination; rather, it is the journey toward becoming better educators and humans. We are bound to stumble, to make mistakes in the classroom and life, but it is in these moments that our capacity for growth is made clear. Mistakes, after all, are the stepping stones toward growth. Yet, in our mistakes, we must hold ourselves accountable to change.

In this book, we have also invited you to lean into the spirit of vulnerability. Vulnerability is hard to accept in a world that often requires perfectionism. In her TED Talk (2010), Brené Brown says, "Staying vulnerable is a risk we have to take if we want to experience connection." As teachers, we want to feel connected to our students. Connection is more often than not a reason why many of us chose to enter the education profession. There were connections to school, learning, content, and people. We, Jacobē and Reshma, have tried to lean into vulnerability as much as possible to build a connection with you. We have aired some of our missteps as educators in the hopes that you might experience a sense of empathy. We are not speaking to you from a place of power or privileged positionality. We want you to know that we are human, and as humans, we are unintentionally conditioned in ways that prompt us to make errors. What matters is how we choose to move forward.

We invite you to join us in moving beyond our current systems and classrooms and consider the profound potential that lies beyond the well-trodden path we know well. When we move beyond the known, fear, an uninvited companion, may cast shadows on the road ahead. Yet, it is precisely in acknowledging and understanding fear that we find the catalyst for transformative change. To move beyond fear, we must first recognize its presence. Fear is not an adversary but a guidepost, signaling that we could be on the verge of something significant. As we embark on this journey together, let us be mindful that fear is a natural companion on the path of innovation. It is not the absence of fear that defines us but our ability to navigate fear with courage and resilience. Together, let us move beyond the status quo by using authenticity as a vehicle toward liberation, as a testament to our unwavering belief that a better future exists.

To have grace for oneself is to acknowledge the inherent complexity of change. It is an acceptance that, in this intricate dance of transformation, missteps, and challenges are not only anticipated but inherent. Granting ourselves the gift of grace allows for the recognition of our efforts, even when the outcomes are not what we envisioned. It is an act of self-compassion that fuels resilience and provides the emotional fortitude necessary to navigate the uncertainties of change.

To this end, dear reader, we wish you the absolute happiness and luck as you continue on your journey to be the educator that your students need—the one that you needed.

With love and solidarity,

Jacobē and Reshma

REFERENCES AND RESOURCES

The Afrofuture Strategies Institute. (n.d.). *Frequently asked questions*. Accessed at www.afrofuturestrategies.com/faq on August 20, 2024.

Akkerman, S. F., & Meijer, P. C. (2011). A dialogical approach to conceptualizing teacher identity. *Teaching and Teacher Education*, 27(2), 308–319.

Alexander, M. (2012). *The new Jim Crow: Mass incarceration in the age of colorblindness*. New York: New Press.

Alexie, S. (2017). *The absolutely true diary of a part-time Indian* (10th anniversary ed.). New York: Little, Brown.

Alsubaie, M. A. (2015). Hidden curriculum as one of current issue of curriculum. *Journal of Education and Practice*, 6(33), 125–128.

American Psychological Association. (n.d.). *Trauma*. Accessed at www.apa.org /topics/trauma on August 16, 2024.

Annamma, S. A., Connor, D., & Ferri, B. (2013). Dis/ability critical race studies (DisCrit): Theorizing at the intersections of race and dis/ability. *Race Ethnicity and Education*, 16(1), 1–31. https://doi.org/10.1080/13613324.2012.730511

The Annie E. Casey Foundation. (n.d.). *Unequal opportunities in education*. Baltimore, MD: Author. Accessed at https://assets.aecf.org/m/resourcedoc /aecf-racemattersEDUCATION-2006.pdf on March 27, 2023.

Anyon, J. (1980). Social class and the hidden curriculum of work. *Journal of Education*, 162(1), 67–92. https://doi.org/10.1177/002205748016200106

Association of Public and Land-Grant Universities. (n.d.). *How does a college degree improve graduates' employment and earnings potential?* Accessed at www.aplu.org /our-work/4-policy-and-advocacy/publicuvalues/employment-earnings on August 19, 2024.

Au, W. (2011). Teaching under the new Taylorism: High-stakes testing and the standardization of the 21st century curriculum. *Journal of Curriculum Studies*, *43*(1), 25–45. https://doi.org/10.1080/00220272.2010.521261

Azevedo, L. (2018). Race talk and the conspiracy of silence: Understanding and facilitating difficult dialogues on race. *Public Integrity*, *20*(4), 419–422. https://doi.org/10.1080/10999922.2017.1403221

Baines, A. D. (2014). *(Un)learning disability. Recognizing and changing restrictive views of student ability.* New York: Teachers College Press.

Baines, A., Medina, D., & Healy, C. (2023). *Amplify student voices: Equitable practices to build confidence in the classroom.* Arlington, VA: ASCD.

Baker-Bell, A. (2020). *Linguistic justice: Black language, literacy, identity, and pedagogy.* New York: Routledge.

Bakhtin, M. M. (1990). *Art and answerability: Early philosophical essays* (M. Holquist & V. Liapunov, Eds.). Austin: University of Texas Press.

Baldwin, J. (1963). *The fire next time.* New York: Dial Press.

Bamdad, N., & Misra, S. (2020, August 14). *Centering equity in intermediary relationships: An opportunity for funders.* Washington, DC: Change Elemental. Accessed at https://changeelemental.org/wp-content/uploads/2020/08 /Centering_Equity_Intermediary_report_WEB.pdf on August 20, 2024.

Barnum, M. (2018, March 23). *Race, not just poverty, shapes who graduates in America—and other education lessons from a big new study.* Accessed at www.chalkbeat.org/2018/3/23/21104601/race-not-just-poverty-shapes-who -graduates-in-america-and-other-education-lessons-from-a-big-new-stu on March 27, 2023.

Barthes, R. (2012). *Mythologies* (R. Howard & A. Lavers, Trans.). New York: Hill and Wang. (Original work published 1957)

Bell, J. (2022, December). Don't ignore emotions in equity work—embrace them. *Learning Forward*, *43*(6), 30–34.

Bell, J. (2023). Creating humanizing homeplaces as a way to embrace and protect my Blackness. In K. Porcher, R. Ramkellawan-Arteaga, C. Hinds-Rodgers, & J. Bell (Eds.), *From being woke to doing #theWork: Using culturally relevant practices to support student achievement and sociopolitical consciousness* (pp. 33–47). Boston: BRILL. https://doi.org/10.1163/9789004544734

Betts, F. (1992, November 1). *How systems thinking applies to education.* Accessed at https://ascd.org/el/articles/how-systems-thinking-applies-to-education on August 19, 2024.

Beyoncé (Director & Writer). (2020). *Black is king* [Film]. Burbank, CA: Walt Disney Pictures; Parkwood Entertainment.

Bivens, D. (1995). *Internalized racism: A definition*. Accessed at https://supportnewyork.files.wordpress.com/2018/04/internalizedracism.pdf on August 19, 2024.

Bivens, D. (2005). What is internalized racism? In M. Potapchuk, S. Leiderman, D. Bivens, & B. Major (Eds.), *Flipping the script: White privilege and community building* (pp. 43–51). Silver Spring, MD: MP Associates and the Center for Assessment and Policy Development. Accessed at www.mpassociates.us/uploads/3/7/1/0/37103967/flippingthescriptmostupdated.pdf on August 19, 2024.

Boston University. (n.d.). *Teaching the hidden curriculum*. Accessed at www.bu.edu/teaching-writing/resources/teaching-the-hidden-curriculum on November 13, 2024.

Bowles, S., & Gintis, H. (2011). *Schooling in capitalist America: Educational reform and the contradictions of economic life*. Chicago: Haymarket Books.

Britzman, D. P. (2003). *Practice makes practice: A critical study of learning to teach* (Rev. ed.). Albany: State University of New York Press.

Brookhart, S. M. (2013). Classroom assessment in the context of motivation theory and research. In J. H. McMillan (Ed.), *SAGE handbook of research on classroom assessment* (pp. 35–54). Thousand Oaks, CA: SAGE. https://doi.org/10.4135/9781452218649

brown, a. m. (2017). *Emergent strategy: Shaping change, changing worlds*. Chico, CA: AK Press.

Brown v. Board of Education of Topeka, 347 U.S. 483 (1954).

Brown, B. (2010, June). *The power of vulnerability* [Video]. TED Conferences. Accessed at www.ted.com/talks/brene_brown_the_power_of_vulnerability on September 23, 2024.

Bryk, A. S. (2010). Organizing schools for improvement. *Phi Delta Kappan*, 91(7), 23–30.

Bryk, A. S. (2020, August 11). *Learning to improve*. Accessed at https://ssir.org/books/excerpts/entry/learning_to_improve on August 19, 2024.

Bryk, A. S., Gomez, L. M., Grunow, A., & LeMahieu, P. G. (2015). *Learning to improve: How America's schools can get better at getting better*. Cambridge, MA: Harvard Education Press.

Butler, O. E. (1979). *Kindred*. Doubleday.

Butler, O. E. (2000, May). A few rules for predicting the future. *Essence*, *31*(1), 165–264.

CAN TV. (2016, November 21). *Engineered conflict* [Video file]. Accessed at www.youtube.com/watch?v=F7BeOUXMSro on October 21, 2022.

The Center for Culturally Proficient Educational Practice. (n.d.). *The continuum*. Accessed at https://ccpep.org/home/what-is-cultural-proficiency/the -continuum on October 30, 2023.

Christian, L. (2021, March 22). *How to be your authentic self: 7 powerful strategies to be true* [Blog post]. Accessed at https://soulsalt.com/how-to-be-your -authentic-self on August 19, 2024.

Coates, T.-N. (2015). *Between the world and me*. Spiegel & Grau.

Collins, P. H. (2000). *Black feminist thought: Knowledge, consciousness, and the politics of empowerment* (2nd ed.). New York: Routledge.

Collins, P. H. (2006). "Intersecting Oppressions." Accessed at https://us.sagepub .com/sites/default/files/upm-binaries/13299_Chapter_16_Web_Byte_Patricia _Hill_Collins.pdf on November 18, 2024.

Coogler, R. (Director). (2018). *Black panther* [Film]. Burbank, CA: Marvel Studios.

Crenshaw, K. (1989). Demarginalizing the intersection of race and sex: A black feminist critique of antidiscrimination doctrine, feminist theory and antiracist policies. *University of Chicago Legal Forum*, *19*(1), 139–167.

Crenshaw, K. (1991). Mapping the margins: Intersectionality, identity politics, and violence against women of color. *Stanford Law Review*, *43*(6), 1241–1299. https://doi.org/10.2307/1229039

Crompton, C. J., Hallett, S., Axbey, H., McAuliffe, C., & Cebula, K. (2023). "Someone like-minded in a big place": Autistic young adults' attitudes towards autistic peer support in mainstream education. *Autism*, *27*(1), 76–91. https://doi.org/10.1177/13623613221081189

CultureContent. (2012, June 20). *Toni Morrison refuses to privilege White people in her novels!* [Video file]. Accessed at www.youtube.com/watch?v=F4vIGvKpT1c on August 20, 2024.

The Daily Show. (2021, February 18). *Heather McGhee—"The Sum of Us" and the true cost of racism* [Video file]. Accessed at www.youtube.com/watch?v =IZpse-90KTY on August 20, 2024.

Danielewicz, J. (2001). *Teaching selves: Identity, pedagogy, and teacher education*. Albany: State University of New York Press.

Darder, A. (2012). *Culture and power in the classroom: Educational foundations for the schooling of bicultural students* (20th anniversary ed.). Boulder, CO: Paradigm.

Darling-Hammond, L. (1998, March 1). *Unequal opportunity: Race and education.* Accessed at www.brookings.edu/articles/unequal-opportunity-race-and-education on March 29, 2023.

Davis, A. Y. (2012). *The meaning of freedom: And other difficult dialogues.* San Francisco: City Lights Books.

De Bruyckere, P., & Kirschner, P. A. (2016). Authentic teachers: Student criteria perceiving authenticity of teachers. *Cogent Education, 3*(1), Article 1247609. https://doi.org/10.1080/2331186X.2016.1247609

Delpit, L. (2006). *Other people's children: Cultural conflict in the classroom.* New York: New Press.

DiAngelo, R. (2018). *White fragility: Why it's so hard for White people to talk about racism.* Boston: Beacon Press.

Divergent Perspectives. (2022, March 13). *We need to talk about ableism in education* [Blog post]. Accessed at www.divergentperspectives.co.uk/post/we-need-to-talk-about-ableism-in-education on May 10, 2023.

Doxie, M. R. (2021). *Addressing the institutional systemic trauma of teachers in K–12 educational environments: Hope for the wounded professional* [Doctoral dissertation, Mills College]. Ann Arbor, MI: ProQuest Dissertations & Theses. www.proquest.com/openview/464b9c71e132276c530b3d110e6d4a95/1?pq-origsite=gscholar&cbl=18750&diss=y

Duff, P. A., & Uchida, Y. (1997). The negotiation of teachers' sociocultural identities and practices in postsecondary EFL classrooms. *TESOL Quarterly, 31*(3), 451–486.

The Editors of Encyclopaedia Britannica. (2024, July 6). *Positive-sum game.* Accessed at www.britannica.com/topic/positive-sum-game on August 21, 2024.

Elliott, G. (2016, July 21). *10 ways White supremacy wounds White people: A tale of mutuality.* Accessed at https://afsc.org/news/10-ways-white-supremacy-wounds-white-people-tale-mutuality on October 23, 2023.

Emdin, C. (2016). *For White folks who teach in the hood . . . and the rest of y'all too: Reality pedagogy and urban education.* Boston: Beacon Press.

Emdin, C. (2021a). Foreword. In S. Safir & J. Dugan (Eds.), *Street data: A next-generation model for equity, pedagogy, and school transformation* (pp. xi–xiv). Thousand Oaks, CA: Corwin.

Emdin, C. (2021b). *Ratchetdemic: Reimagining academic success*. Boston: Beacon Press.

Fallace, T., & Fantozzi, V. (2013). Was there really a social efficiency doctrine? The uses and abuses of an idea in educational history. *Educational Researcher, 42*(3), 142–150.

Fecho, B. (2013). Globalization, localization, uncertainty and wobble: Implications for education. *International Journal for Dialogical Sciences, 7*(1), 115–128.

Fecho, B., & Botzakis, S. (2007). Feasts of becoming: Imaging a literacy classroom based on dialogic beliefs. *Journal of Adolescent and Adult Literacy*, X(7), 548–558.

Fitzpatrick, A. (2018, April 20). *It's not just* Black Panther. *Afrofuturism is having a moment*. Accessed at https://time.com/5246675/black-panther-afrofuturism on March 17, 2023.

Flum, H., & Kaplan, A. (2012). Identity formation in educational settings: A contextualized view of theory and research in practice. *Contemporary Educational Psychology, 37*(3), 240–245. https://doi.org/10.1016/j.cedpsych.2012.01.003

Flynn, A. K. (n.d.). *The science of skin color* [Video file]. Accessed at https://ed.ted.com/lessons/the-science-of-skin-color-angela-koine-flynn on April 18, 2023.

Freire, P. (2000). *Pedagogy of the oppressed* (M. B. Ramos, Trans.; 30th anniversary ed.). New York: Continuum. (Original work published 1968)

Gee, J. P. (2015). *Social linguistics and literacies: Ideology in discourses* (5th ed.). New York: Routledge.

Givens, J. R. (2021). *Fugitive pedagogy: Carter G. Woodson and the art of Black teaching*. Cambridge, MA: Harvard University Press.

Gold, M. (2018, June 21). *The ABCs of L.G.B.T.Q.I.A.+*. Accessed at www.nytimes.com/2018/06/21/style/lgbtq-gender-language.html on August 7, 2024.

Gorski, P. (2020, October 1). *How trauma-informed are we, really?* Accessed at www.ascd.org/el/articles/how-trauma-informed-are-we-really on May 10, 2023.

Gray, D. L., Hope, E. C., & Byrd, C. M. (2020). Why Black adolescents are vulnerable at school and how schools can provide opportunities to belong to fix it. *Policy Insights From the Behavioral and Brain Sciences, 7*(1). https://doi.org/10.1177/2372732219868744

Gray, P. (2013, August 26). *School is a prison—and damaging our kids.* Accessed at www.salon.com/2013/08/26/school_is_a_prison_and_damaging_our_kids on February 26, 2023.

Greene, P. (2019, November 12). *White flight, without the actual flight.* Accessed at www.forbes.com/sites/petergreene/2019/11/12/white-flight-without-the -actual-flight on April 19, 2023.

Hammond, Z. (2015a). *Culturally responsive teaching and the brain: Promoting authentic engagement and rigor among culturally and linguistically diverse students.* Thousand Oaks, CA: Corwin.

Hammond, Z. (2015b, February 26). *Making CRT manageable* [Blog post]. Accessed at https://crtandthebrain.com/making-crt-manageable on October 23, 2022.

Hansberry, L. (1994). *A raisin in the sun.* New York: Vintage Books.

Hansen, M. (2021, May 18). *The U.S. education system isn't giving students what employers need.* Accessed at https://hbr.org/2021/05/the-u-s-education-system -isnt-giving-students-what-employers-need on August 7, 2024.

Harro, B. (2000). The cycle of socialization. In M. Adams, W. J. Blumenfeld, R. Castañeda, H. W. Hackman, M. L. Peters, & X. Zúñiga (Eds.), *Readings for diversity and social justice* (pp. 15–21). New York: Routledge.

Hartman, S. (2019). *Wayward lives, beautiful experiments: Intimate histories of riotous Black girls, troublesome women, and queer radicals.* New York: Norton.

Harvard Library. (n.d.). *Education.* Accessed at https://library.harvard.edu /confronting-anti-black-racism/education on April 18, 2023.

Harvard T. H. Chan School of Public Health. (n.d.). *Understanding unconscious bias.* Accessed at www.hsph.harvard.edu/wp-content/uploads/sites/2597 /2022/06/Types-of-Bias-Ways-to-Manage-Bias_HANDOUT-1.pdf on June 19, 2023.

Headlee, C. (Host). (2013, August 20). Is it time to get rid of IQ tests in schools? [News-talk program episode]. In *Tell me more.* Accessed at www.npr.org /2013/08/20/213822184/is-it-time-to-get-rid-of-iq-tests-in-schools on October 31, 2023.

High Tech High Unboxed [Producer]. (2024, October 2). What improvers can learn from civil rights organizers [Podcast episode]. High Tech High Unboxed. Accessed at https://hthunboxed.org/podcasts/what-improvers-can-learn-from -civil-rights-organizers on November 13, 2024.

Hinds-Rodgers, C. (2023). The healing of a nation. In K. Porcher, R. Ramkellawan-Arteaga, C. Hinds-Rodgers, & J. Bell (Eds.), *From being woke to doing #theWork: Using culturally relevant practices to support student achievement and sociopolitical consciousness* (pp. 111–124). Boston: BRILL. https://doi.org/10.1163/9789004544734

hooks, b. (1994). *Teaching to transgress: Education as the practice of freedom.* New York: Routledge.

The Ignant Intellectual [theignantintellectual]. (2021, July 21). *People from the hood are bombarded with the ideology that we have made it when we LEAVE THE PLACES THAT* [Photograph]. Instagram. www.instagram.com/p /CRmtweQLHq6/?utm_medium=copy_link

Ingersoll, R. M., & Tran, H. (2023, October 30). *The rural teacher shortage.* Accessed at https://kappanonline.org/rural-teacher-shortage-ingersoll-tran on August 6, 2024.

Jin, C. H. (2021, May 25). *6 charts that dismantle the trope of Asian Americans as a model minority.* Accessed at www.npr.org/2021/05/25/999874296/6-charts -that-dismantle-the-trope-of-asian-americans-as-a-model-minority on August 20, 2024.

Joffe-Walt, C. (Host). (2020). *Nice White parents* [Audio podcast]. The New York Times. Accessed at www.nytimes.com/2020/07/23/podcasts/nice-white -parents-serial.html on March 29, 2023.

Kelley, J., Sansfaçon, A. P., Gelly, M. A., Chiniara, L., & Chadi, N. (2022). School factors strongly impact transgender and non-binary youths' well-being. *Children, 9*(10), 1520.

Kendall, F. (2013). *Understanding White privilege: Creating pathways to authentic relationships across race* (2nd ed.). New York: Routledge.

Kendi, I. X. (2019). *How to be an antiracist.* New York: One World.

Kendi, I. X. (2023). *Stamped from the beginning: The definitive history of racist ideas in America.* New York: Bold Type Books.

Kraft, M. A., & Lyon, M. A. (2024). The rise and fall of the teaching profession: Prestige, interest, preparation, and satisfaction over the last half century. *American Educational Research Journal, 0*(0). https://doi.org/10.3102 /00028312241276856

Lalor, A. D. M. (2012). Keeping the destination in mind. *Educational Leadership, 70*(1), 75–78.

Lalor, A. D. M. (2017). *Ensuring high-quality curriculum: How to design, revise, or adopt curriculum aligned to student success.* Alexandria, VA: ASCD.

The Leading Through Learning Playbook. (n.d.). *Knowledge management.* Accessed at www.leadingthroughlearning.org/knowledge-management on February 2, 2023.

Lemov, D. (2010). *Teach like a champion: 49 techniques that put students on the path to college.* San Francisco: Jossey-Bass.

Lloyd, C. M., Carlson, J., & Alvira-Hammond, M. (2021, March 5). *Federal policies can address the impact of structural racism on Black families' access to early care and education.* Accessed at www.childtrends.org/publications/federal -policies-can-address-the-impact-of-structural-racism-on-black-families-access -to-early-care-and-education on April 18, 2023.

Love, B. L. (2019). *We want to do more than survive: Abolitionist teaching and the pursuit of educational freedom.* Boston: Beacon Press.

Lyiscott, J. (2019). *Black appetite, White food: Issues of race, voice, and justice within and beyond the classroom.* New York: Routledge.

Martin, J. L., & Brooks, J. N. (2020). Turning White: Co-opting a profession through the myth of progress, an intersectional historical perspective of Brown v. Board of Education. *Intersectionality and the History of Education, 45*(2). https://doi.org/10.4148/0146-9282.2190

Maslow, A. H. (1943). A theory of human motivation. *Psychological Review, 50*(4), 370–396. https://doi.org/10.1037/h0054346

Mayfield, V. (2020). *Cultural competence now: 56 exercises to help educators understand and challenge bias, racism, and privilege.* Alexandria, VA: ASCD.

McCarthy, M., & Carter, R. (1994). *Language as discourse: Perspectives for language teaching.* New York: Longman.

McGhee, H. C. (2021). *The sum of us: What racism costs everyone and how we can prosper together.* New York: One World.

Mehta, J., & Allen, R. (Hosts). (2023, May 9). The importance of the land— Learning from Indigenous cultures [Audio podcast episode]. In *Free range humans.* Accessed at https://free-range-humans.simplecast.com/episodes /52-nisgaa-9B_zl2yN on August 20, 2024.

Menakem, R. (2017). *My grandmother's hands: Racialized trauma and the pathway to mending our hearts and bodies.* Las Vegas, NV: Central Recovery Press.

Milder, S. (2018). *Improvement science handbook*. New York: New York City Department of Education. Accessed at www.weteachnyc.org/media2016 /filer_public/76/97/7697a2de-ee3c-4a60-81fc-563bdf1c36d0/nycdoe _improvement_science_handbook_2018_online.pdf on March 14, 2024.

Milner, H. R. (2003). Teacher reflection and race in cultural contexts: History, meanings, and methods in teaching. *Theory Into Practice*, *42*(3), 173–180.

Milner, H. R. (2018, February 1). *Confronting inequity / assessment for equity*. Accessed at www.ascd.org/el/articles/assessment-for-equity on March 26, 2023.

Monáe, J. (2018). *Dirty computer* [Album]. Bad Boy Records.

Morris, M.W. (2018). *Pushout: The criminalization of Black girls in schools*. The New Press.

Morrison, T. (2008). *A mercy*. New York: Knopf.

Muhammad, G. (2020). *Cultivating genius: An equity framework for culturally and historically responsive literacy*. New York: Scholastic.

Muhammad, G. (2023). *Unearthing joy: A guide to culturally and historically responsive teaching and learning*. New York: Scholastic.

Natanson, H. (2023, March 17). *Few legal challenges to laws limiting lessons on race, gender*. Accessed at www.washingtonpost.com/education/2023/03/17/legal -challenges-gender-critical-race-theory on April 18, 2023.

The National Commission on Excellence in Education. (1983, April). *A nation at risk: The imperative for educational reform*. Washington, DC: Author. Accessed at http://edreform.com/wp-content/uploads/2013/02/A_Nation _At_Risk_1983.pdf on March 28, 2023.

National Education Association. (n.d.). *What you need to know about Florida's "don't say gay" and "don't say they" laws, book bans, and other curricula restrictions*. Accessed at www.nea.org/sites/default/files/2023-06/30424-know-your-rights _web_v4.pdf on December 15, 2023.

Neebe, D., & Sikora, S. (2022, January 27). *What students have to say about improving engagement*. Accessed at www.ascd.org/el/articles/what-students -have-to-say-about-improving-engagement on March 27, 2023.

Neem, J. N. (2017). *Democracy's schools: The rise of public education in America*. Baltimore, MD: John Hopkins University Press.

Nelson, L., & Lind, D. (2015, October 27). *The school-to-prison pipeline, explained*. Accessed at www.vox.com/2015/2/24/8101289/school-discipline-race on August 20, 2024.

The New School for Social Research. (2016, April 10). *Anwar Shaikh publishes an important economic analysis of modern capitalism.* Accessed at http://socialresearchmatters.org/anwar-shaikh-and-an-economic-analysis-of-modern-capitalism on February 2, 2023.

Nittle, N. K. (2021, February 28). *How racism affects children of color in public schools.* Accessed at www.thoughtco.com/how-racism-affects-public-school-minorities-4025361 on March 27, 2023.

Okun, T. (n.d.). *What is White supremacy culture?* [Blog post]. Accessed at www.whitesupremacyculture.info/what-is-it.html on October 23, 2023.

Oleś, P. K., Brinthaupt, T. M., Dier, R., & Polak, D. (2020). Types of inner dialogues and functions of self-talk: Comparisons and implications. *Frontiers in Psychology, 11.* https://doi.org/10.3389/fpsyg.2020.00227

Oluo, I. (2018). *So you want to talk about race.* New York: Seal Press.

Partnership for the Future of Learning. (2022, September 23). *Yolanda Sealy-Ruiz: The archaeology of the self* [Video file]. Accessed at www.youtube.com/watch?v=mmST_lehb_U on August 20, 2024.

PBS. (n.d.). What is race? Accessed at www.pbs.org/race/001_WhatIsRace/001_00-home.htm on April 18, 2023.

Petty, S., & Leach, M. (2020, July 15). *Systems change and deep equity: Pathways toward sustainable impact, beyond "eureka!," unawareness and unwitting harm.* Accessed at https://changeelemental.org/resources/systems-change-and-deep-equity-monograph on August 20, 2024.

Plessy v. Ferguson, 163 U.S. 537 (1896).

Pondiscio, R. (2022, October 11). *What's next for New York charter schools?* Accessed at www.educationnext.org/what-next-for-new-york-charter-schools on August 6, 2024.

powell, j. a. (n.d.). *Challenging racialized structures and moving toward social justice.* Accessed at https://drive.google.com/file/d/1kRiPWN5PqGVofDxmCuKUmzQf0EhQ6TGL/view on August 20, 2024.

Prejudice. (2023, November 15). In *APA dictionary of psychology.* Accessed at https://dictionary.apa.org/prejudice on August 16, 2024.

Ramkellawan-Arteaga, R. (2017). *Literary literacies: An examination of literacy practices in an urban New York City charter school.* Ann Arbor, MI: ProQuest Dissertations & Theses.

Ramkellawan-Arteaga, R. (2020). Making the leap: Rethinking assessment practices in schools. In C. Martin, D. Polly, & R. Lambert (Eds.), *Handbook of research on formative assessment in pre-K through elementary classrooms* (pp. 1–17). Hershey, PA: IGI Global.

Ramkellawan-Arteaga, R. (2023). Get right to do right. In K. Porcher, R. Ramkellawan-Arteaga, C. Hinds-Rodgers, & J. Bell (Eds.), *From being woke to doing #theWork: Using culturally relevant practices to support student achievement and sociopolitical consciousness* (pp. 59–68). Boston: BRILL. https://doi.org/10.1163/9789004544734

Ray, R., & Gibbons, A. (2021, November). *Why are states banning critical race theory?* Accessed at www.brookings.edu/blog/fixgov/2021/07/02/why-are -states-banning-critical-race-theory on April 18, 2023.

Reddy, A. (2008). The eugenic origins of IQ testing: Implications for post-Atkins litigation. *DePaul Law Review, 57*(3), 667–677.

Reill, A. (2023, December 5). *A simple way to make better decisions.* Accessed at https://hbr.org/2023/12/a-simple-way-to-make-better-decisions on August 7, 2024.

Rogin, M. (2022). *Change starts with me: Talking about race in the elementary classroom.* Bloomington, IN: Solution Tree Press.

Rothstein, R. (2017). *The color of law: A forgotten history of how our government segregated America.* New York: Liveright.

Safir, S., & Dugan, J. (2021). *Street data: A next-generation model for equity, pedagogy, and school transformation.* Thousand Oaks, CA: Corwin.

Salazar, M. del C. (2013). A humanizing pedagogy: Reinventing the principles and practice of education as a journey toward liberation. *Review of Research in Education, 37*(1), 121–148. https://doi.org/10.3102/0091732X12464032

Sealey-Ruiz, Y. (2021). *Racial literacy: A policy research brief produced by the James R. Squire Office of the National Council of Teachers of English.* Champaign, IL: National Council of Teachers of English. Accessed at https://ncte.org /wp-content/uploads/2021/04/SquireOfficePolicyBrief_RacialLiteracy _April2021.pdf on August 20, 2024.

Sealey-Ruiz, Y. (n.d.). *Arch of self.* Accessed at www.yolandasealeyruiz.com /archofself on September 27, 2021.

Shaikh, A. (2016). *Capitalism: Competition, conflict, crises.* New York: Oxford University Press.

Simmons, D. (2021, March 1). *Why SEL alone isn't enough*. Accessed at www.ascd
.org/el/articles/why-sel-alone-isnt-enough on March 29, 2023.

Sokolower, J. (2013, June 4). *Schools and the New Jim Crow: An interview with
Michelle Alexander*. Accessed at https://truthout.org/articles/schools-and-the
-new-jim-crow-an-interview-with-michelle-alexander on May 16, 2023.

Sousa, D. A., & Tomlinson, C. A. (2018). *Differentiation and the brain: How
neuroscience supports the learner-friendly classroom* (2nd ed.). Bloomington, IN:
Solution Tree Press.

Staples, G. B. (2019, November 22). *Pushout: Making the case to stop criminalizing
Black girls*. Accessed at www.ajc.com/lifestyles/pushout-making-the-case-stop
-criminalizing-black-girls/FNbaSCXlhFkQwypWgfeFFM on March 28, 2023.

Steinskog, E. (2018). *Afrofuturism and Black sound studies: Culture, technology, and
things to come*. New York: Palgrave Macmillan.

Stembridge, A. (2020). *Culturally responsive education in the classroom: An equity
framework for pedagogy*. New York: Routledge.

Stern, A. M. (2016, January 7). *That time the United States sterilized 60,000 of its
citizens*. Accessed at www.huffpost.com/entry/sterilization-united-states_n
_568f35f2e4b0c8beacf68713 on January 31, 2023.

Stivers, M. (2021, June 30). *How capitalism undermines progressive education
reform*. Accessed at https://jacobin.com/2021/06/schooling-in-capitalist
-america-progressive-education-reform on March 27, 2023.

Stockton University. (n.d.). *About Sankofa*. Accessed at www.stockton.edu/sankofa
/about.html on October 2, 2023.

Storey, J. (2006). *Cultural theory and popular culture: An introduction* (4th ed.).
Athens: University of Georgia Press.

Stubbs, R. (2019, April 17). *A wrestler was forced to cut his dreadlocks before a
match. His town is still looking for answers*. Accessed at www.washingtonpost
.com/sports/2019/04/17/wrestler-was-forced-cut-his-dreadlocks-before-match
-his-town-is-still-looking-answers on March 28, 2023.

Sue, D. W. (2015). *Race talk and the conspiracy of silence: Understanding and
facilitating difficult dialogues on race*. Hoboken, NJ: Wiley.

Tatum, B. D. (2017). *"Why are all the black kids sitting together in the cafeteria?"
And other conversations about race* (3rd ed.). New York: Basic Books.

Taubman, P. M. (2012). *Disavowed knowledge: Psychoanalysis, education, and
teaching*. New York: Routledge.

Tomlinson, C.A. (2014). *The differentiated classroom: Responding to the needs of all learners.* (2nd ed.). Alexandria, VA: ASCD.

Tourmaline. (2020, July 2). *Filmmaker and activist Tourmaline on how to freedom dream.* Accessed at www.vogue.com/article/filmmaker-and-activist-tourmaline-on-how-to-freedom-dream on February 12, 2023.

Truong, D. (2022, May 17). *Detracking in K–12 classrooms.* Accessed at www.usnews.com/education/k12/articles/detracking-in-k-12-classrooms on March 28, 2023.

United States Congress. (2001). *No Child Left Behind Act of 2001.* Public Law 107-110.

U.S. Department of Education. (2015). *Every Student Succeeds Act (ESSA).* Accessed at www.ed.gov/essa on September 23, 2024.

U.S. National Commission on Excellence in Education. (1983). *A nation at risk: The imperative for educational reform.* Washington, D.C.: Author.

Valle, J. W., & Connor, D. J. (2019). *Rethinking disability: A disability studies approach to inclusive practices* (2nd ed.). New York: Routledge.

Van Dyken, N. (2017). *Everyday narcissism: Yours, mine, and ours.* Las Vegas, NV: Central Recovery Press.

van Loon, R. (2017). *Creating organizational value through dialogical leadership: Boiling rice in still water.* Cham, Switzerland: Springer International.

Wiliam, D. (2018). *Embedded formative assessment* (2nd ed.). Bloomington, IN: Solution Tree Press.

Winn, M. T. (2018). *Justice on both sides: Transforming education through restorative justice.* Cambridge, MA: Harvard Education Press.

Winn, M. T. (2021). Futures matter: Creating just futures in this age of hyper-incarceration. *Peabody Journal of Education, 96*(5), 527–539.

Womack, Y. L. (2013). *Afrofuturism: The world of Black sci-fi and fantasy culture.* Chicago: Chicago Review Press.

Young, M. D. (1958). *The rise of the meritocracy, 1870–2033.* London: Thames and Hudson.

INDEX

W

White students and culture
  and an example of synthesis
    between sociopolitical systems
    and schools, 57
  and harm, 115, 116, 121, 122
  and identities, 91
  and intersectionality, 30, 45
  and socialization, 27
White supremacy
  and curriculum, 152
  and an example of synthesis
    between sociopolitical systems
    and schools, 57
  and habits of being, 155, 156

and harm, 123
and looking back to move
  forward, 4
methods and sources of, 150
and social activism, 125
Winn, M., 125, 129
Womack, Y., 142–143
word cloud exploring teachers'
  mindsets around teaching, 149

Z

zero-sum thinking
  as a barrier to change, 70–72
  transcending, 73–75
zero-tolerance policies, 67

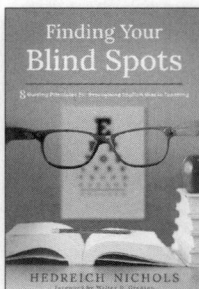

Finding Your Blind Spots
Hedreich Nichols
Author Hedreich Nichols infuses this book with a direct, yet conversational style to help you identify biases that adversely affect your practice and learn how to move beyond those biases to ensure a more equitable, inclusive campus culture.
BKG022

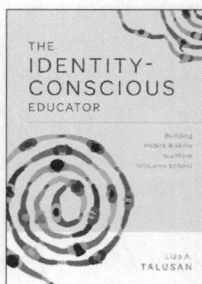

The Identity-Conscious Educator
Liza A. Talusan
Learn powerful, practical strategies for creating an inclusive school community and engaging in meaningful conversations to make this work successful. *The Identity-Conscious Educator* provides a framework for building awareness and understanding of five identity categories: race, social class, gender, sexual orientation, and disability.
BKG031

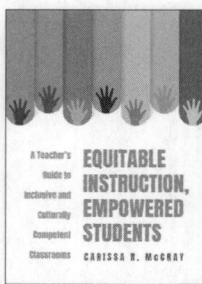

Equitable Instruction, Empowered Students
Carissa R. McCray
Learn practical strategies for ensuring each of your students feels valued, welcomed, and empowered. Author Carissa R. McCray provides the tools to combat biases inherent in education with pedagogy that encourages students to dismantle the injustices surrounding them.
BKG036

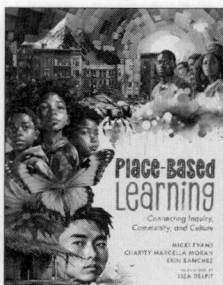

Place-Based Learning
Micki Evans, Charity Marcella Moran, and Erin Sanchez
Understand the impact a sense of place has on education, culture, and community. The authors share seven place-based learning design principles and how to smoothly implement place-based learning projects using their project-planning tool, community asset map, and other resources.
BKG106

Solution Tree | Press
a division of
Solution Tree

Visit SolutionTree.com or call 800.733.6786 to order.